Teaching Emergent Readers

Teaching Emergent Readers

Collaborative Library Lesson Plans

Judy Sauerteig

LIBRARIES UNLIMITED

A Member of the Greenwood Publishing Group

Westport, Connecticut • London

Library of Congress Cataloging-in-Publication Data

Sauerteig, Judy.
    Teaching emergent readers : collaborative library lesson plans / by Judy Sauerteig.
        p. cm.
    Includes bibliographical references and index.
    ISBN 1-59158-251-2 (pbk. : alk. paper)
    1. Children's literature—Study and teaching (Primary) 2. Children—Books and reading—Bibliography. 3.
School libraries—Activity programs. 4. Reading (Primary) I. Title.
Z1037.A1S247 2005
372.41'2—dc22   2005016099

British Library Cataloguing in Publication Data is available.

Library of Congress Catalog Card Number: 2005016099
ISBN: 1-59158-251-2

First published in 2005

Libraries Unlimited, 88 Post Road West, Westport, CT 06881
A Member of the Greenwood Publishing Group, Inc.
www.lu.com

Printed in the United States of America

The paper used in this book complies with the
Permanent Paper Standard issued by the National
Information Standards Organization (Z39.48–1984).

10 9 8 7 6 5 4 3 2 1

Dedicated to the students, teachers,
and staff at

Cherry Creek Academy,
Englewood, Colorado

Contents

Introduction

Nothing is more exciting to teachers and parents than to hear a child exclaim, "I can read this whole book all by myself!" The culmination of teaching reading to young children is the enjoyment they discover when they become independent readers.

Teaching Emergent Readers: Collaborative Library Lesson Plans is a book designed to use popular beginning readers to motivate students, make connections with the classroom and library, review skills, and expand understanding. The plans include activities for the media specialist or librarian to introduce the books, activities for the teacher to use before and after reading the text, writing opportunities, and a letter to parents explaining the lessons that have been taught and suggesting enrichment activities to use at home. In this way, the student, teacher, media specialist, and parents are all focused on the same book, which will allow the student to make connections that enhance comprehension.

Another helpful connection found in this volume is the suggestions for using the books for character education. The situations and characters are easy for students to identify with, allowing teachers and parents to have discussions about character issues in connection with the literature.

Phonics, phonemic awareness, and decoding have also been included in the lesson plans. Depending on students' reading abilities, the teacher may want to use all of these skill sections or just the ones that are appropriate for the individual or group.

The comprehension questions and writing activities can be used as a complete lesson or as a starting point, adding other activities to develop skills appropriate to the student or group.

The books listed on the parent page are also a resource for the teacher and librarian. Some lend themselves to an author study. Others follow a theme that can be a part of the beginning reader lesson plan. The possibilities for study and activities between the library and the classroom are limitless. Enjoy and let your students celebrate their own "independence day" as they discover the joys of independent reading.

And I Mean It, Stanley

by Crosby Bonsall
Reading Level 1.2

Setting:	The yard of Stanley the Dog
Characters:	A little boy, Stanley the Dog, and a cat
Plot:	Stanley is on the other side of the fence, and a little boy really wants him to come out and play, but Stanley will not. So the little boy pretends he does not care and tries to entice Stanley by telling him he is building something wonderful.
Solution:	Finally, Stanley comes bounding out from behind the fence and makes a terrible mess but the little boy is still happy to have his friend back.
Summary:	A little boy is sitting on his front step waiting for his dog, Stanley, to appear. The boy becomes impatient and finally starts yelling at Stanley to come out from behind the fence. When Stanley won't come, the boy tells him he doesn't care and says that he will play without him. He begins building a "special thing." The entire time he does this, however, he continues to yell at Stanley, saying he doesn't want Stanley to come out anymore. He says, "And I mean it, Stanley." Finally, Stanley does come out and destroys the thing the little boy built, but all is forgiven in the end.
Curriculum Connections:	Pet unit, character education—forgiveness

ACTIVITIES FOR MEDIA SPECIALISTS

Schema

Ask students, "Has anyone ever had friends come to play who won't play what you want them to?" Let the children tell their stories, but without using any names. Ask what they did in this situation.

Predicting

Show students the drawing on the cover of the book and have them look closely at the little boy's face. Ask the children, "Does he look happy? How do you think he feels? Who do you think Stanley is?" Show the title page and the pages that follow, and have the students pay special attention to the little boy. How do his actions change? Ask them what they think is the problem.

Visualizing

In the picture on the title page, there is a big barrel with an assortment of junk. Have the students close their eyes and picture something they could make with the junk.

Library Skills

Discuss the title page and the information found there. Explain why it is important to look at all the pages at the beginning of a book. Pictures can tell part of the story.

ACTIVITIES FOR TEACHERS

Decoding

Students may need to review or decode some of the following words in the story.

listen	fence	myself	having	really
truly	making	peek	hear	neat

Phonics

Review the three sounds of /ea/ with the following words:

Long e: mean neat bead lead

Short e: head bread dread instead

Long a: great break steak

Phonemic Awareness

Play the thumbs-up game. Children will put their thumbs up when they hear a sound that you have selected for them to review. Check to make sure everyone is looking at you and not at the other children to ensure that they are not getting clues from a classmate.

Comprehension

Recall

What is the little boy waiting for in the first few pages before the story begins? *He is waiting for Stanley the Dog.*

Why does he say he can play by himself? *He thinks it will make the dog feel bad and come out to play.*

When the little boy says, "I am having a lot of fun. A lot of fun!" does he look as if he really is having fun? *No, he looks sad.*

The little boy feels better and his mood changes when he has an idea. What is the idea? *To build something with the junk he found.*

What does the cat doing during the story? *The cat tries to catch the bird.*

Why does the little boy yell through the crack in the fence again? *Because he really wants Stanley to come out and see the really neat thing that he built.*

Inferring

Why do you think the little boy looks so angry after he peeks through the fence? *The dog won't come out from behind the fence.*

How do you think the cat feels about the dog? *Accept any reasonable answer.*

Synthesizing

Have students find some old things that nobody wants and see what they can create with them. Remind them to be sure to ask permission before taking something.

WRITING ACTIVITIES

Main Idea

Write the main idea of the story in one sentence.

_____

_____

_____

Sequencing

Number the following events in the order they happened in the story.

_____ The little boy tells Stanley not to peek.

_____ Stanley licks the little boy's face.

_____ The really great thing is all finished.

_____ The little boy is making a really great thing.

_____ The little boy tells Stanley he doesn't need him.

Story Elements

Who is the main character? _____

Where does the story take place? _____

What is the problem? _____

How is the problem solved? _____

Compare and Contrast

Compare the cat to the dog. How are they alike? How are they different?

_____

_____

_____

Summarizing

Write a summary of the story on another piece of paper.

PARENTS' PAGE

Dear Parents,

We have just finished reading *And I Mean It, Stanley* by Crosby Bonsall. The story begins with a little boy sitting on his front step, waiting for his dog, Stanley, to appear. The boy becomes impatient and finally starts yelling at Stanley to come out from behind the fence. When Stanley won't come, the boy tells him he doesn't care and says that he will play without him. He begins building a "special thing." The entire time he does this, however, he continues to yell at Stanley, saying he doesn't want Stanley to come out anymore. He says, "And I mean it, Stanley." Finally, Stanley does come out and destroys the thing the little boy built, but all is forgiven in the end. The following activities will enhance your child's learning experience.

Enrichment Activities

This little boy has a very good imagination. He dresses up in costumes just for the fun of it. This would be a good time to start a costume box. See what you can find around the house. It's so much fun to dress up! There will be an abundance of laughter in the house with this activity.

Help your child find some old things that are no longer of any use, and let him or her build something. See how many different "things" your child can build. Just like the little boy in the book, the creation does not have to be beautiful—it just has to be fun to do.

The following books may be of interest:

> *Glue and Go Costumes for Kids* by Holly Cleeland
>
> *Costumes* by Lola M. Schaefer

The following books are about other big, fun dogs:

> *Pinkerton, Behave!* by Steven Kellogg
>
> *A Rose for Pinkerton* by Steven Kellogg
>
> *Tallyho, Pinkerton!* by Steven Kellogg
>
> *Prehistoric Pinkerton* by Steven Kellogg
>
> *A Penguin Pup for Pinkerton* by Steven Kellogg
>
> *Clifford the Big Red Dog* by Norman Bridwell
>
> *Clifford's Puppy Days* by Norman Bridwell
>
> *Clifford's Christmas* by Norman Bridwell
>
> *Clifford's Thanksgiving Visit* by Norman Bridwell

Have your child write a story about or draw a picture of another big, mischievous dog.

Aunt Eater Loves a Mystery

by Doug Cushman
Reading Level 2.7

Setting: A train, a friend's house, and Aunt Eater's house.

Characters: Aunt Eater, her friend Eliza, and Mr. Chumley

Plot: Aunt Eater finds mystery wherever she goes.

Solution: Aunt Eater always solves the mysteries by thinking and reasoning.

Summary: In this chapter book, Aunt Eater the anteater travels on a train to visit her friend Eliza. There is a mystery to solve on the train, at Eliza's house, when Aunt Eater returns home, and again when she agrees to take care of her neighbor's cat.

Curriculum Connections: Mystery writing, transportation unit, friendship unit

---

ACTIVITIES FOR MEDIA SPECIALISTS

Schema

Ask children if they have ever heard of an animal called a giant anteater. Show a picture of an anteater and ask the children if they know why this animal might be good at eating ants. *Anteaters, Sloths, and Armadillos* by Ann O. Squire is a possible nonfiction book to use.

Discuss the elements of a mystery, including *suspense, a hook, danger and risk, foreshadowing, cliffhangers to keep us reading, and strong characters.*

Predicting

Read the chapter titles. Have the students try to predict what might happen in each chapter. Remind them to keep in mind that this is a mystery story.

Visualizing

Ask students to do the following exercise: Picture yourself riding on a train, and all of a sudden you hear loud popping sounds. How would you feel? What would you do?

Ask students: Have you ever made popcorn before? Can you explain what happens?

Library Skills

Ask students the following questions:

How would you find a mystery in the library, even though they are written by many different authors?

Does your library use special stickers to help you find mysteries?

Do mysteries always have to be scary to be fun to read?

ACTIVITIES FOR TEACHERS

Decoding

Before reading, have students decode the following words:

conductor	embarrassed
switched	exciting
disappeared	figure
stammered	laundromat
muttered	tingled

Phonics

Have students write words with short /o/ as in "pop."

cop	hop	mop	top
clop	flop	slop	shop
stop	plop	drop	glop

Phonemic Awareness

Orally blend a beginning sound with the /ain/ pattern to make a new word.

r-ain	tr-ain	p-ain	ch-ain
dr-ain	g-ain	m-ain	v-ain

Comprehension

Recall

In the chapter "Aunt Eater Rides the Train," why did everyone run to the front of the train? *They heard a lot of popping coming from that direction.*

Why did Aunt Eater take popcorn in her suitcase? *Eliza loved popcorn!*

Who owned the bag with all the tools inside? *The engineer of the train.*

Inferring

Why do you think Aunt Eater always finds a mystery wherever she goes?

Why do you think Aunt Eater thought her neighbor, Mr. Chumley, was being robbed? What was the mistake in her thinking?

Where do you think Aunt Eater's "latest mystery book" came from?

Synthesizing

Have students plan a mystery of their own. Tell them to try it out on a friend to see if they can figure it out, giving some clues as to where something is hidden.

WRITING ACTIVITIES

Main Idea

Write the main idea of the story in one sentence.

_____

_____

_____

Sequencing

Number the following events in the order they happened in the story.

_____ Aunt Eater gets a mystery book in the mail.

_____ Aunt Eater's bag is stolen on the train.

_____ Aunt Eater and Sam read a book.

_____ Aunt Eater solves the mystery of the shadow.

_____ Popcorn pops all over the engine car.

Story Elements

Who is the main character? _____

Where does the story take place? _____

What is the problem? _____

How is the problem solved? _____

Compare and Contrast

Compare Mr. Chumley and the mailman. How are they alike? How are they different?

Summarizing

Write a summary of the story on another piece of paper.

PARENTS' PAGE

Dear Parents,

We have just finished reading *Aunt Eater Loves a Mystery* by Doug Cushman. The Aunt Eater character is a fictional giant anteater. She loves mystery stories and is always reading them. Everything she does seems to turn into a mystery! There are four chapters in this book. Aunt Eater travels on a train to visit her friend Eliza. There are mysteries to solve on the train, at Eliza's house, when Aunt Eater returns home, and again when she agrees to take care of her neighbor's cat. Your child may wish to reread part or all of the book. While reading, encourage your reader to use expression in her or his voice.

The following activities will further enhance your child's learning experience.

Enrichment Activities

If your child has never ridden on a train, try to go to a place where you can see a train. We do not use this a mode of transportation as much as we did in the past, but children often find it very enchanting.

Check out a train book from the library such as the following:

Henry Hikes to Fitchburg by Donald B. Johnson

The Caboose Who Got Loose by Bill Peet

Mr. Putter and Tabby Take the Train by Cynthia Rylant

The Little Engine That Could by Watty Piper

Train—Eyewitness Books by John Coiley

A few more fun activities to consider:

Visit a train or model-train museum or a train station.

Line up your kitchen chairs in a row and pretend you are on a train. Your child's stuffed animals can be the passengers.

Have your child make up his or her own mystery story.

Children enjoy making shapes with shadows. Shine a bright light against a wall and see what shapes you and your child can create with your hands. These can also be traced onto paper.

Have your child draw a picture or write about a real or make-believe train.

Aunt Eater's Mystery Vacation

by Doug Cushman
Reading Level 2.7

Setting:	A ferry boat and the Hotel Bathwater
Characters:	Aunt Eater, Mr. Bundy (the hotel detective), Pat the Mynah Bird, Professor Slagbottom, Edna Herring (the mystery writer)
Plot:	Aunt Eater tries to create a mystery out of everything that happens.
Solution:	Aunt Eater uses many clues to solve the mysteries.
Summary:	In this four-chapter book, Aunt Eater takes a ferry, which hits rough waters and tosses the captain overboard. After rescuing the captain, she is on her way to the Hotel Bathwater for rest and relaxation. But a thief is lurking about, and she has mysteries to solve.
Curriculum Connections:	Mystery stories, writing unit

ACTIVITIES FOR MEDIA SPECIALISTS

Schema

Ask students: Has anyone here ever lost something? Of course—we all have. How many of you have lost something and then found it again? (Pick a few children to tell their tale.) These are examples of a mysteries.

How many have ever been on a ferry boat? (If none of your students have, then explain or show a picture of a ferry boat.)

Predicting

Ask students to think about the title of the book. What kinds of events might happen on a mystery vacation?

Visualizing

Ask students to do the following exercise: Close your eyes. Pretend that you are on a boat. The water is very smooth, and the trip is pleasant. Then all of a sudden, the wind starts to blow, the waves get bigger and bigger, and the boat starts to rock. Show me what you would be doing.

Library Skills

Ask students how they would find more mysteries in a library. Explain that some libraries put stickers on the books to show a mystery. They can also put the keyword "mystery" in the computer to find more mysteries or they can ask a librarian.

The Aunt Eater books are a series. Question the children to see if they know what "series" means. Show them the other books in this series: *Aunt Eater Loves a Mystery, Aunt Eater's Mystery Halloween,* and *Aunt Eater's Mystery Christmas*

ACTIVITIES FOR TEACHERS

Decoding

The students may need to review or decode some of these words from the story:

passengers	moaned	anchor
collection	squawked	diamond
windowsill	package	complain

Phonics

Have students find words that have the short /e/ sound as in "bell."

Phonemic Awareness

See if students can recognize little words in compound words:

overboard	bathwater	everyone	notebook
anywhere	anyone	lifeboats	cupboard
bellhop	footprints	someone	everywhere
hallway	bathroom	windowsill	everything

Comprehension

Recall

How was the captain of the ferry boat saved from falling in the water? *He grabbed the anchor.*

Who had stolen the diamond ring from Mrs. Wainscot? *The mynah bird.*

What did the mystery writer lose in Chapter Four?

Inferring

In Chapter One, why did everyone look sick? *The boat was swaying back and forth.*

Why do you think the Aunt Eater was suspicious of the women who went in the back door of the hotel in Chapter Four? *Because of the word "sneak."*

In Chapter Two, why do you think Aunt Eater dreamed about "a dark figure that left giant footprints"? *Because she was probably reading about it in her mystery book.*

Synthesizing

Have your students do the following activity: If you were a detective on a television program, what would you call yourself? Create a character. Tell what kind of special abilities or talents this character would have. How would he or she go about solving crimes? What would be the character's "secret weapon"? Write a mystery or draw a cartoon-type story about your character.

WRITING ACTIVITIES

Main Idea

Write the main idea of the story in one sentence.

_____

_____

_____

Sequencing

Number the following events in the order they happened in the story.

_____ Aunt Eater finds an ending to the mystery writer's story.

_____ A woman in a green dress loses her diamond ring.

_____ Aunt Eater boards a ferry to the Hotel Bathwater.

_____ The captain of the ferry falls overboard.

_____ A rare bone goes missing.

Story Elements

Who is the main character? _____

Where does the story take place? _____

What is the problem? _____

How is the problem solved? _____

Compare and Contrast

Compare Mr. Bundy the hotel manager and Professor Slagbottom. How are they alike? How are they different?

_____

_____

_____

Summarizing

Write a summary of the story on another piece of paper.

PARENTS' PAGE

Dear Parents,

We have just finished reading a book titled *Aunt Eater's Mystery Vacation*. It is a book with four chapters. Aunt Eater just wants to have a nice restful vacation and read her mystery books. But as hard as she tries, she is always interrupted by someone who has a problem or a mystery to be solved. She begins her vacation by rescuing the captain of a ferry boat. Then she solves the mystery of the missing diamond ring by following an unraveling sweater to the thief. In Chapter Three, Professor Slagbottom misplaces his rare dinosaur bone that somehow ended up in the soup in the hotel kitchen. The last chapter is about an ending to a story that has been lost, and, of course, Aunt Eater saves the day once again. The following activities will enhance the story and solidify your child's learning experience.

Enrichment Activities

If possible, show your child a ferry boat. If not, use a picture book such as *Boat Book* by Gail Gibbons.

Have your child retell his or her favorite chapter in the book. If it is difficult for your child to put events in order orally, he or she can write or draw pictures to show the sequence of events.

Have your child write or tell a story about when he or she lost something.

The following books in this series by Doug Cushman may be of interest to your child:

Aunt Eater Loves a Mystery

Aunt Eater's Mystery Halloween

Aunt Eater's Mystery Christmas

The following mystery stories may also be of interest.

Cam Jansen series by David Adler

Nate the Great series by Marjorie W. Sharmat

The Case of the Double Cross by Crosby N. Bonsall

Have your child write about or draw a picture of a favorite character in the book.

Biscuit Goes to School

by Alyssa S. Capucilli
Reading Level 1.0

Setting: Biscuit's home and school

Characters: Biscuit the puppy and his master

Plot: Biscuit the puppy wants to go to school with his master, a little girl.

Solution: Biscuit finds his way to school, and everyone really likes him.

Summary: Biscuit's little master leaves for school on the school bus, and she insists that Biscuit cannot go to school with her. Biscuit goes to the pond, the park, the gym, and the library to find her. Finally, he finds her in the school cafeteria. She tries to hide Biscuit, but the teacher and the kids see him and fall in love with him. Even the teacher wants him to stay at school for the day.

Curriculum Connections: Pet Day—Many schools have a pet day either in kindergarten or first grade. This would be a great book to read before that special day.

ACTIVITIES FOR MEDIA SPECIALISTS

Schema

Ask the students: How many of you have a dog or puppy? Has that pet ever followed you when you didn't want him or her to? What did you do? The girl in this story has the same problem.

Predicting

Show the students the picture on the cover of the book. Ask the following questions: Why do you think the puppy is pulling on the strap of the backpack? What do you think is the puppy's name?

Visualizing

Ask students to do the following exercise: Close your eyes and picture a puppy in the classroom. Do you think it would be easy to do your work if there were a puppy here? Which would you rather do, play with the puppy or do your schoolwork?

Library Skills

Discuss the following with students: If I go to the computer catalog and type the keyword "dog," I will get hundreds of returns—that is, titles that have something to do with dogs. How would you organize the titles to choose ones in which you are interested? (Discuss fiction and nonfiction titles and how the student can tell the difference by looking at the computer screen.)

ACTIVITIES FOR TEACHERS

Decoding

The students may need to review or decode the following words from the story:

stay	woof	go	going
pond	park	play	story
snack	doing	come	comes
meet	like	likes	everyone

Phonics

Review the /oo/ sound as in "school."

school	woof	soon	spoon
loon	moon	noon	spool

Phonemic Awareness

Read a few sentences in the book and have the students clap out the number of words in the sentences. Ask them how many words they hear.

Comprehension

Recall

What did the little girl tell the puppy when she got on the bus? *Dogs don't go to school.*

Did Biscuit stay home? *No.*

Where did Biscuit go? *He went to the pond, park, school, gym, library, and cafeteria.*

Why was the little girl so upset when she saw the puppy in the cafeteria? *Dogs are not supposed to go to school.*

Where did the little girl hide the puppy? *In her backpack.*

Inferring

How do you think Biscuit found the school? *He followed the bus or he followed his nose. (Accept any reasonable answers.)*

Why do you think the little boy in the library was telling the puppy to *shhhh!*? *The library is supposed to be a quiet place.*

Synthesizing

Describe some ways that Biscuit could play and keep busy during the day while his master is at school.

WRITING ACTIVITIES

Main Idea

Write the main idea of the story in one sentence.

_____

_____

_____

Sequencing

Number the following events in the order they happened in the story.

_____ Biscuit escapes from the backpack.

_____ Biscuit walks in the door of the school.

_____ The teacher holds Biscuit on his lap.

_____ The little girl gets on the school bus.

_____ The little girl sees Biscuit in the cafeteria.

Story Elements

Who are the main characters? _____

Where does the story take place? _____

What is the problem? _____

How is the problem solved? _____

Compare and Contrast

Compare Biscuit to Clifford the Big Red Dog. How are they alike? How are they different?

_____

_____

_____

Summarizing

Write a summary of the story on another piece of paper.

PARENTS' PAGE

Dear Parents,

We have just finished reading the book *Biscuit Goes to School* by Alyssa S. Capucilli. Biscuit's little master, a young girl, leaves for school on the school bus, and she insists that Biscuit cannot go to school with her. Biscuit goes to the pond, the park, the gym, and the library to find her. Finally, he finds her in the school cafeteria. She tries to hide Biscuit, but the teacher and the kids see him and fall in love with him. Even the teacher wants him to stay at school for the day. The following activities will enhance your child's learning experience.

Enrichment Activities

Pet stores are always fun to visit to watch all the little puppies. Humane societies also have puppies and kittens. Most children would love to have a pet, but sometimes it isn't possible, so volunteering at an animal shelter may be a way to give your child the experience without actually owning a pet.

This is also a good time to discuss safety around animals that your child does not know. Explain that we cannot always be sure that a pet will be friendly to everyone.

Help your child write a story about a puppy.

Have your child retell this story to you or someone else in the family.

The following books about puppies and dogs may be of interest to your child.

Fiction

Clifford the Big Red Dog series by Norman Bridwell

Pinkerton series by Steven Kellogg

Henry and Mudge series by Cynthia Rylant

Just Me and My Puppy by Mercer Mayer

Arthur's Pet Business by Marc Brown

Arthur's New Puppy by Marc Brown

Harry the Dirty Dog by Gene Zion

Nonfiction

Puppies Are Like That by Jan Pfloog

Puppies by Scott Carey

Puppies by Zuza Vrbova

The Boston Coffee Party

by Doreen Rappaport
Reading Level 2.7

Setting: Colonial Boston during the Revolutionary War

Characters: Mrs. Homans, Sarah Homans, Emma Homans, Merchant Thomas, and the women in the town

Plot: Greedy Merchant Thomas is warehousing coffee until there is none at the other merchants, and then he charges extremely high prices for his coffee.

Solution: The women of Boston teach Merchant Thomas a lesson using events similar to those of the historic Boston Tea Party.

Summary: During the Revolutionary War, times are hard in colonial Boston. Greedy Merchant Thomas is overcharging for sugar. Then he locks up all the coffee so he can overcharge for that, too! Young Sarah Homans wants to teach him a lesson. Merchant Thomas is about to attend a party he won't soon forget!

Curriculum Connections: Revolutionary War unit, patriotism, Fourth of July

ACTIVITIES FOR MEDIA SPECIALISTS

Schema

Ask the students if they know what caused the Revolutionary War. If they do not know anything about the war, then explain it briefly and talk about the Fourth of July.

Ask the students if they know of a time when something was expensive because it was very popular and many people wanted it—for example, a toy or game.

Predicting

Show students the picture and title on the cover. Ask: What do you think the girls are doing, and what does the title mean?

Ask students: Chapter 2 is called the "Sewing Party." The women and girls are sewing two hundred shirts that are exactly alike. Who do you think might be wearing these shirts?

Library Skills

Who is the author of this book? *Doreen Rappaport.*

Is this a true story? Could it be true? (Point out the information at the end of the book.)

Discuss historical fiction.

ACTIVITIES FOR TEACHERS

Decoding

The students may need to review or decode some of the following words in the story.

merchant	charge	charges
shillings	listening	patterns
barrels	harbor	business
cobblestone	warehouse	daughters

Phonics

Have students find words in the story with the /ch/ and /tch/ phonograms. Have students find words in the story with the /ed/ ending.

Phonemic Awareness

Give each child three index cards with the letters B, M, and E written on one card each. Choose a sound. Tell the children to hold up the B card if they hear the sound at the beginning of the word, the M card if they hear the sound in the middle of the word, and E card if they hear the sound at the end of the word.

Choose words from the book to use in practicing oral blending. Say each sound separately and have the children put them altogether to pronounce the whole word.

Comprehension

Recall

Why did Mother need the sugar? *To make jam.*

What did greedy Merchant Thomas do with the forty barrels of coffee? *He locked them up in his warehouse.* Why? *So that when coffee was scarce, he could charge more for it.*

Who came up with the idea to have a coffee party? *Sarah did.* Was it like a tea party? *Not really.*

How did the ladies get the key to the warehouse? *They bounced Merchant Thomas down the street in a cart until he finally gave them the key.*

Inferring

What do you think Mrs. Homans meant when she said, "Not as sorry as you will be when our men return from the war"?

Do you think Merchant Thomas was helping to support the soldiers who were fighting the war?

Synthesizing

Explain that when groups are protesting, they often chant a slogan to tell people what it is they want to change. Create a chant for the women as they marched to the warehouse.

Read a book about the Boston Tea Party and compare the two "parties."

WRITING ACTIVITIES

Main Idea

Write the main idea of the story in one sentence.

_____

_____

_____

Sequencing

Number the following events in the order they happened in the story.

_____ The women of Boston take Merchant Thomas for a bumpy ride.

_____ The women fill pots and pans with coffee.

_____ Aunt Harriet says Merchant Thomas must be punished for being greedy.

_____ Emma and Sarah go to the shop for some sugar.

_____ The girls sew notes to the soldiers into their shirts.

Story Elements

Who are the main characters? _____

Where does the story take place? _____

What is the problem? _____

How is the problem solved? _____

Compare and Contrast

Compare Aunt Harriet and Mrs. Homans. How are they alike? How are they different?

_____

_____

_____

_____

Summarizing

Write a summary of the story on another piece of paper.

PARENTS' PAGE

Dear Parent,

We have just finished reading a book titled *The Boston Coffee Party*. It is a story about women and girls in Boston at home during the Revolutionary War who are trying to help the soldiers by sewing uniforms for them. Everything is scarce during the war. One greedy merchant in town is hording sugar and coffee and charging very high prices for them. The women of the town decide this is not fair and organize their own "Boston Coffee Party." You can imagine what happens to the greedy merchant! The following activities will enhance your child's learning experience.

Enrichment Activities

Make a bonnet like the one the girls and women are wearing by cutting a round piece of material, cutting slits around the edge, running a drawstring through the slits, and pulling to gather the material. Tie a bow in the front.

Measure out a cup, a pound, a tablespoon, and so on of sugar. Show your child a five-pound bag. How big is the barrel? Find an example around the house. Many people have half barrels for flower containers.

Discuss how shortages make items more expensive.

Read other books about the Revolutionary War, such as:

> *Boston Tea Party* by Pamela Duncan Edwards
>
> *The 18 Penny Goose* by Sally M. Walker
>
> Biographies of George Washington, Paul Revere, William Dawes, Molly Pitcher, Nathan Hale

Have your child write about or draw a picture of a favorite part of the story.

Buffalo Bill and the Pony Express

by Eleanor Coerr
Reading Level 2.7

Setting: The Old West in 1860

Characters: Buffalo Bill Cody, Pony Express Bosses, and Riders

Plot: Bill must endure many problems and dangers as a rider.

Solution: Bill uses quick wit and training as a young man to be successful.

Summary: In this chapter book about young Buffalo Bill Cody, Bill, seeking adventure, wants to be a rider for the Pony Express. At age sixteen, he proves he can do the job and is hired. The book tells about the dangers and adventures of riding in the Wild West.

ACTIVITIES FOR MEDIA SPECIALISTS

Schema

Ask the students the following questions:

What can you tell me about horses?

What do you know about the country west of the Mississippi River? (Point out the region on a map.)

Have you ever been to a museum, a western ranch, or a house that was built in the Old West?

Predicting

Ask students: What kinds of dangers and challenges might have awaited a lone rider in the Wild West?

Visualizing

Ask students to do the following exercises: Picture yourself riding a horse as fast as you can and imagine how you would feel after riding all night long.

Think about a time when you have been outside in a thunderstorm. What did that feel like?

Library Skills

Ask students: Do you think this is a true story? Why or why not?

Explain to the students that Buffalo Bill Cody was a real person and that some of the events in the story could have happened, but some events may not be true. We call this type of book historical fiction.

Discuss other works of historical fiction.

Where would one look to find a true (nonfiction) book about Buffalo Bill Cody?

ACTIVITIES FOR TEACHERS

Decoding

The students may need to review or decode some of the following words in the story:

spunk   deliver   stagecoaches
flannel   neckerchief   hoofbeats
stationmaster thieves   sheriff

Phonics

Starting with the word "mail," ask students to change the beginning sound to make new words. How many can they make?

Fluency

Have the students read the letters home that Bill writes to Ma. Remind them that it is like talking to her and should be read with expression.

Read aloud the first eight pages, ending with Bill saying, "I'm not afraid." Read with expression, and then let the students act out the scene.

Comprehension

Recall

Between which two cities did the Pony Express deliver mail? *It delivered mail between St. Joseph, Missouri, and Sacramento, California.*

How far is it from St. Joseph to Sacramento? *It is 2,000 miles.*

Explain how the mail was delivered to people along the Pony Express route.

Inferring

Why doesn't Bill tell his mother exactly what is happening to him on his rides from Red Buttes to Three Crossings?

Why do you think Buffalo Bill was the best and bravest?

Synthesizing

Why do you think Bill's mother did not question what Bill was doing or ask what his life in the Pony Express was like?

Tell about a time when you were really, really tired, just like Bill was when he finished riding two legs of the trip.

Retelling

Tell what happened in Chapter 4, "The Shoot Out." Remember to tell it in the order it happened.

WRITING ACTIVITIES

Main Idea

Write the main idea of the story in one sentence.

_____

_____

_____

Sequencing

Number the following events in the order they happened in the story.

_____ Bill sees a sign for a job.

_____ Mr. Majors gives Bill the job.

_____ Bill is chased by a pack of wolves.

_____ Bill has to make a double run because one of the riders is sick.

_____ Bill talks to the chief about the outlaws.

Story Elements

Who are the main characters? _____

Where does the story take place? _____

What is the problem? _____

How is the problem solved? _____

Compare and Contrast

Compare Mr. Majors and the chief. How are they alike? How are they different?

_____

_____

_____

Summarizing

Write a summary of the story on another piece of paper.

PARENTS' PAGE

Dear Parents,

We have just finished reading *Buffalo Bill and the Pony Express.* We have talked about what it would be like to live in the Old West, where there were only horses and carriages or wagons for transportation. We have talked about some of the words that may be unfamiliar to your child and discussed their meaning. The following activities will reinforce the learning and help your child to remember vocabulary and connect what has been learned.

Enrichment Activities

Try to communicate using some form of signing like the early settlers had to do when they encountered Native Americans.

Watch an old western movie together. Talk about which parts are fiction and which are truly representative of the Old West.

Read other books about Buffalo Bill Cody. Look in the biography section of your library.

Talk about the bravest thing your child or you have ever done. What does it mean to be brave?

If your child has never ridden a horse, it would be a wonderful experience.

Have your child draw pictures of four of the most important events in the story.

Cave Boy

by Cathy East Dubowski and Mark Dubowski
Reading Level 1.6

Setting:	Harry's family's cave
Characters:	Harry and Chief Grump
Plot:	Harry wants to make Chief Grump smile.
Solution:	Harry invents something that does make Chief Grump smile.
Summary:	Harry is a prehistoric boy who lives with his family in a cave. He loves to play and make a lot of noise. Chief Grump, however, does not appreciate the noise Harry makes. When it is time for Chief Grump's birthday, Harry wants to make him something new to cheer him up. He makes something, but no one knows what it is—even Harry. But when the gift is presented to Chief Grump, the chief figures it out by accident.
Curriculum Connections:	Prehistoric unit, the discovery of fire, the beginnings of humans, the invention of the the wheel

ACTIVITIES FOR MEDIA SPECIALISTS

Schema

Study the cover of the book, then ask students the following questions: What is the boy doing? What are the markings on the rocks? Do you think this boy is living in our time? When do you think he lived? What do you know about cave people? Did they live at the same time as the dinosaurs?

Predicting

Have the students predict how a cave boy might play. How would he create artwork? How would he make music? What would he eat?

Visualizing

Ask students to do the following exercise: Close your eyes and pretend that you are living in a cave. What would you look like? How would you dress? What would you eat? How would you get your food? What would you do for fun?

Library Skills

On the cover of the book, the cave boy is stacking rock blocks. The pictures on the blocks give us some clues about the plants and animals that lived at the time. How would we be able to find out more about the plants and animals that lived during this time period?

ACTIVITIES FOR TEACHERS

Decoding

The students may need to review or decode some of the following words from the story:

swing	climb	ever
before	hammer	boomer
chief	grump	tomorrow
surprise	presents	guess

Phonics

Have the students start with the word "boy" and change the beginning sound to make other words that rhyme, such as, *toy, soy, coy, joy, Roy, Troy*

Phonemic Awareness

Blend the following sounds and have the students repeat the whole word:

b-a-n	c-a-n	f-a-n
t-a-n	p-a-n	v-a-n
m-a-n	r-a-n	D-a-n

Comprehension

Recall

What did cave boy like to do "most of all"? *He liked to make new things.*

What did cave boy make when he put a rock on top of a stick? *A bammer or hammer.*

In the book, whose birthday was the next day? *It is Chief Grump's birthday.*

What did cave boy invent? *The wheel.*

Inferring

Why didn't anyone know what the cave boy had made to give to Chief Grump? *They had never seen a wheel before.*

Why do you think people bought the chief presents for his birthday, even though he was always mad? *Because he was the chief, and they had to show respect.*

How do you think all the people felt when Chief Grump threw their presents down the hill? *They probably felt sad and bewildered.* How can you tell? *By the looks on their faces.*

What do you think might happen now that cave boy has made a tricycle? *Let the students name other things that have been invented with wheels.*

Synthesizing

Write a story about Chief Grump now that he is happy. How would things in the tribe change?

WRITING ACTIVITIES

Main Idea

Write the main idea of the story in one sentence.

_____

_____

_____

Sequencing

Number the following events in the order they happened in the story.

_____ Chief Grump has a birthday party.

_____ Cave boy makes a tricycle.

_____ Cave boy makes a bammer.

_____ Chief Grump kicks the birthday present down the hill.

_____ Cave boy makes a boomer.

Story Elements

Who are the main characters? _____

Where does the story take place? _____

What is the problem? _____

How is the problem solved? _____

Compare and Contrast

Compare cave boy to his friends. How are they alike? How are they different?

_____

_____

_____

Summarizing

Write a summary of the story on another piece of paper.

PARENTS' PAGE

Dear Parents,

We have just finished reading a book titled *Cave Boy*. It is about a boy who loves to make things. He wants to make something for Chief Grump's birthday that will make him happy because the chief always seems to be mad. Cave Boy *does* make something, but nobody knows what it is until Chief Grump kicks it down the hill and it rolls. Now Cave Boy knows what to make! The tricycle that the boy creates finally makes the chief smile. The following activities will enhance your child's learning experience.

Enrichment Activities

Visit a museum of Natural History where your child can observe the skeletons or dioramas of prehistoric animals and relics.

Use picture writing to write notes to each other or to friends. You can find examples of picture writing on the cover of *Cave Boy* or in other resources at the library.

Take a camping trip, even to the backyard or a park, and try to figure out how to find shelter and food like Cave Boy.

Check out nonfiction books on prehistoric life such as the following:

Prehistoric Rock Art by Marinella Terzi

The Stone Age by Patricia D. Netzley

Wild and Woolly Mammoth by Aliki

Help your child design a toy that you can make from rocks or natural materials.

Have your child imagine living in the times of Cave Boy and write a story or draw a picture about the adventures he or she might have in that day and age.

Chang's Paper Pony

by Eleanor Coerr
Reading Level 2.8

Setting: The town of Gold Ditch during the Gold Rush years between 1850 and 1864

Characters: Chang, Grandpa Li, and Big Pete

Plot: Chang wants a pony in the worst way—it's all he ever thinks about. But he and his Grandpa are poor and must work very hard. Several times, Chang comes close to solving his problem, but with no luck. Just when he is about to give up, Big Pete comes up with a solution.

Solution: Chang promises to clean Big Pete's cabin if he will take him to the gold fields so he can find gold and buy a pony. His plan does not pan out, but Chang keeps his promise and cleans Big Pete's cabin. When he does, he discovers gold flakes that have fallen into the cracks of the floor and gives them to Pete. Pete then shares the gold and buys a pony for Chang.

Summary: Chang has to help his Grandpa Li in the kitchen of the Gold Ditch Hotel to feed all the miners who have come to strike it rich. All Chang really wants is a horse, but all he has is a picture on the wall of a white pony. Chang is lonesome because there is no one his age to play with. He thinks about how to get a pony all the time, even during his English lessons. The teacher is not nice to him, and the miners tease him about his ponytail and Chinese customs. Big Pete is the only miner who is friendly to him, and Pete eventually helps Chang get his pony.

Curriculum Connections: Immigration unit, westward expansion unit, study of the gold rush

ACTIVITIES FOR MEDIA SPECIALISTS

Schema

Show the book and title to the students. Explain that Chang is from China. Ask the students on which continent China is located. Ask them what they know about China.

Predicting

Have the students predict what they think a paper pony is. Read the five titles of the chapters and let the children try to connect the information they gather from the titles.

Ask the students these questions: Does Chang look like he is in China in the picture on the cover? Where do you think he is?

Visualizing

Ask students to do the following exercise: Picture something you want very, very much. How does that feel? How will you feel if you cannot have it? How will you feel if you work hard to earn it?

Library Skills

Ask the students where they would look in the library if they wanted to learn more about China. See whether the students can search on the computer and find the books about China on the shelves.

ACTIVITIES FOR TEACHERS

Decoding

The students may need to decode or review the following words from the story:

remembered	potatoes	humble	kitchen
tightened	scholar	wiggling	swallowed
pretended	loosened	scooped	blistered
galloped	glittering	whinnied	whispered

Phonics

Review the rules about dropping the silent "e" and doubling the final consonant. Have the children practice adding /ed/ endings to the following words:

stop	stopped	smile	smiled
slap	slapped	tease	teased
scrub	scrubbed	stare	stared
skin	skinned	like	liked

Phonemic Awareness

Have the students orally replace the middle sound in the following words:

stop	step	slap	slip	slop		
stare	store	like	lake			
not	nut	net	hat	hot	hit	hut
well	will	wall	pop	pep	pup	

Fluency

There is an emotional scene when Chang runs into the kitchen to Grandpa Li because the miners are teasing him. This is an important point in the story as well. Have the children read the parts with feeling.

Comprehension

Recall

Why did Grandpa Li and Chang leave China? *There was a war going on.*

Where in America did they land? *San Francisco.*

Where did Chang find gold flakes? *In the cracks in Big Pete's cabin.*

Where did Big Pete take the gold that he discovered and Chang collected? *To a bank in Sacramento.*

Inferring

How will a pony help Chang? *If he has a pony, he will have a friend.*

Why do you think Grandpa Li did not go out to the gold fields? *Because it would be too risky.*

Why do you think Big Pete treated Chang better than the other miners? *He was a better man, or he may have had children of his own.*

Synthesizing

Find a book of Chinese characters. Create a short note with the characters. Try to use a paintbrush and ink or substitute water colors with very little water added.

WRITING ACTIVITIES

Main Idea

Write the main idea of the story in one sentence.

_____

_____

_____

Sequencing

Number the following events in the order they happened in the story.

_____ Chang wants to go home to China because the miners are mean to him.

_____ Big Pete brings Chang a pony.

_____ Big Pete comes to Gold Ditch.

_____ Chang wishes for a pony.

_____ Chang goes with Big Pete to learn how to search for gold.

Story Elements

Who are the main characters? _____

Where does the story take place? _____

What is the problem? _____

How is the problem solved? _____

Compare and Contrast

Compare Big Pete with some of the other miners. How are they alike? How are they different?

_____

_____

_____

Summarizing

Write a summary of the story on another piece of paper.

PARENTS' PAGE

Dear Parents,

We have just finished reading the story *Chang's Paper Pony* by Eleanor Coerr. This story is historical fiction. Chang has to help his Grandpa Li in the kitchen of the Gold Ditch Hotel to feed all the miners who have come to strike it rich. What Chang really wants is a horse, but all he has is a picture on the wall of a white pony. Chang is lonesome because there is no one his age to play with. He thinks about how to get a pony all the time, even during his English lessons. The teacher is not nice to him, and the miners tease him about his ponytail and Chinese customs. Big Pete is the only miner who is friendly to him, and Pete eventually helps Chang get his pony.

The Chinese who worked in the mining camps actually did sweep up the flakes of gold and save them, just as Chang does in this book. The following activities will enhance the story and allow you to share your child's reading experience.

Enrichment Activities

There are Chinese restaurants in most parts of the United States. It would be a great follow-up to take your family to a restaurant decorated in authentic Chinese décor and have your child try to eat with chopsticks. If possible, have some appropriate questions about food, language, or dress ready for your child to ask the people who run the restaurant. Be sure to explain that this is a school activity.

Chang wanted a pony very much. Many children want a horse or pony, but few who live in the city can actually have one, and caring for a pony is a time-consuming job. Even so, there are other ways a child can get to know these interesting animals. This might be a good time to visit a horse stable or go for a trail ride. Talk about how having a pony was not extravagant at the time Chang lived, when people used horses for transportation.

The following books will provide great follow-up stories:

Fiction

Oranges on Golden Mountain by Elizabeth Partridge

Folktales

Seven Chinese Brothers by Margaret Mahey

Ten Suns: A Chinese Legend by Eric A. Kimmel

Nonfiction

Food and Recipes of China by Theresa M. Beatty

I Am Chinese American by Amy Lee

Poetry

My Chinatown: One Year in Poems by Kam Mak

Crocodile and Hen:
A Bakongo Folktale

by Joan M. Lexau
Reading Level 2.2

Setting: The land along the Congo River where it meets the Atlantic Ocean.

Characters: Crocodile, Hen, and Lizard

Plot: Crocodile really wants to eat nice fat Hen, but she is not afraid of him and says they are brother and sister. This is extremely perplexing to Crocodile, and he seeks an answer.

Solution: Lizard explains that they have one thing in common that could make them brother and sister: both crocodiles and chickens lay eggs.

Summary: Hen goes down to the river to look for food, and there she meets Crocodile. Crocodile wants to eat Hen. Hen, however, stands her ground, looks at him strangely, calls him brother, and then walks away. The next day, Hen goes to the river again, and once again Crocodile wants to eat her. But Hen has so little fear that she simply closes her eyes and fluffs up her feathers; Crocodile shuts his mouth and swims away. He still does not understand how they could be brother and sister. On the third day, Hen goes again to the river. Crocodile is determined to eat her this time, but she just drinks the water. He can't bring himself to do it and decides to ask the Wise Old Woman about this. On his way to see her, Crocodile meets Lizard, who explains that hens, crocodiles, and lizards all lay eggs, and so they must be related. Crocodile really doesn't want to be Hen's brother because he would rather eat her, but from this time on, they are friends.

Curriculum Connections: Storytelling unit, Africa unit, folktales

ACTIVITIES FOR MEDIA SPECIALITSTS

Schema

Ask the children what they know about Crocodiles. If there are any misconceptions, have a nonfiction book available to clarify misunderstandings.

Ask students if they have ever seen a crocodile. Explain the differences between alligators and crocodiles.

Predicting

Show students the cover of the book and have them predict what they think the story may be about.

Library Skills

Ask students how they would find more folktales in the library. Explain that there is a special area in the nonfiction section for folktales, fairy tales, tall tales, and legends from around the world.

ACTIVITIES FOR TEACHERS

Decoding

The students may need to review or decode some of the following words:

mouth	brother	surprised	sister
really	fear	fluffed	lives
head	drinks	scales	feathers

Phonics

Review the –ide word family.

wide	side	hide	ride
bride	slide	pride	guide

Phonemic Awareness

Have the students change beginning, middle, and ending sounds to form new words.

hen	pen	den	men	ten
hen	hum	hut	hit	hat
hen	hem	heck		

Comprehension

Recall

The first time Hen met Crocodile, how did she look at him? *With no fear, first with one eye and then the other.*

What did Hen do to show Crocodile she had no fear the second time she went to the river? *She shut her eyes and fluffed up her feathers.*

What did she do the third time? *She put her head down to drink water.*

Why was Crocodile so confused about Hen calling him "brother"? *He did not see how they could be brother and sister because they were not alike in any way.*

What other animals did you see in the pictures besides Hen, Crocodile, and Lizard? *A monkey, a mouse, a giraffe, and a frog.*

Inferring

Why do you think Crocodile just swam away when Hen showed no fear? *It was just so unusual that he was really confused.*

Who do you think the Wise Old Women might be? *Accept any reasonable answer.*

Synthesizing

This story could be told with different characters. Retell the story using different animals and set in a different country.

WRITING ACTIVITIES

Main Idea

Write the main idea of the story in one sentence.

_____

_____

_____

Sequencing

Number the following events in the order they happened in the story.

_____ Crocodile goes to find the Wise Old Woman.

_____ Crocodile and Hen are friends from now on.

_____ Lizard explains that it must be because both crocodiles and chickens lay eggs.

_____ Crocodile does not understand why Hen calls him "brother."

_____ Hen goes to the river to find food.

Story Elements

Who are the main characters?_____

Where does the story take place?_____

What is the problem? _____

How is the problem solved? _____

Compare and Contrast

Compare Crocodile and Lizard. How are they alike? How are they different?

_____

_____

_____

Summarizing

Write a summary of the story on another piece of paper.

PARENTS' PAGE

Dear Parents,

We have just finished reading a book titled *Crocodile and Hen* by Joan M. Lexau, a wonderful example of a story that is easy to remember and retell. In the story, Hen goes down to the river to look for food and meets Crocodile. Crocodile wants to eat Hen very badly. Hen, however, stands her ground, looks at him strangely, calls him brother, and walks away. The next day Hen goes to the river again, and once again Crocodile wants to eat her. But she has so little fear that she closes her eyes and fluffs up her feathers; Crocodile shuts his mouth and swims away. He still doesn't understand how they could be brother and sister. On the third day, Hen goes to the river, Crocodile is determined to eat her, but she just drinks the water. He can't bring himself to do it and decides to ask the Wise Old Woman about this. On his way to see her, Crocodile meets Lizard, who explains that hens, crocodiles, and lizards all lay eggs, and so they must be related. Crocodile really doesn't want to be Hen's brother because he would rather eat her, but from this time on, they are friends. The following activities will enhance your child's learning experience.

Enrichment Activities

This is a great story to practice storytelling. Storytelling is a skill that is useful in the real world; stories can be used to entertain friends, to persuade, and to emphasize a point. When children retell a story, it helps them remember what they have read and thus improves comprehension. As long as the main ideas are not lost, the story can be told in many ways, giving just the basic facts or using abundant embellishment. The following main ideas are necessary to the story *Crocodile and Hen:*

- Hen goes down to the river to find some food.

- Crocodile sees Hen and wants to eat her.

- Hen shows no fear and just stares at Crocodile, first with one eye and then with the other.

- Crocodile is so confused as to why Hen calls him "brother" that he closes his mouth and goes away.

- The next day, Hen goes to the river again and sees Crocodile. Again she shows no fear. She says, "Brother, don't eat me." She shuts her eyes and fluffs her feathers.

- Crocodile again cannot understand why she calls him "brother."

- On the third day, the same thing happens, and Hen shows no fear. She simply says once again, "Brother, don't eat me" and drinks from the river. Crocodile leaves.

- Crocodile goes to seek answers. He encounters Lizard, who suggests that Hen calls him brother because both crocodiles and chickens lay eggs, so they must be related.

- From this time on, Crocodile and Hen are friends.

Tell stories from when you were a child. Children love these stories, especially if it is a story about when the parent made a mistake or did something foolish. Of course, it's always acceptable to embellish your stories!

Danny and the Dinosaur

by Syd Hoff
Reading Level 1.7

Setting: All around the town

Characters: Danny, the dinosaur, the people and children of the town

Plot: Danny went to the museum and saw many wonderful things. He especially liked the dinosaurs and wished he could play with one.

Solution: All of a sudden, Danny hears a voice, and there is a dinosaur that wants to play with him.

Summary: Danny loves dinosaurs! So when one at the museum speaks to him, he is very excited. Danny and the dinosaur embark on a wonderful journey around town. They walk through the city with Danny riding on the dinosaur's back. They amaze a police officer, a dog, and the people in the buildings and on the street. The dinosaur is helpful, too. He becomes a bridge, a bus, and a boat when necessary. He is the best attraction at the zoo, much to the dismay of all the other animals. He is the best playmate Danny has ever had, and Danny wants to keep him. But the dinosaur says he has to go back to the museum. Danny decides this is for the best because there's no room at his house for a dinosaur anyway.

Curriculum Connections: Dinosaur unit, imagination theme, story writing

ACTIVITIES FOR MEDIA SPECIALISTS

Schema

Ask how many children have ever been to a museum. This will get them talking about their own experiences. Ask how many have ever seen a dinosaur skeleton at a museum.

Predicting

Show the students the cover of the book. Ask: Why do you think there is a little boy riding on a dinosaur? Where do you think they might be going?

Visualizing

Have the children do the following exercise: Close your eyes and picture yourself riding on a dinosaur through the streets of a town. What could you see from that high up that you wouldn't be able to see while walking on the sidewalk?

Library Skills

Ask students where they would look to find a true (nonfiction) book about dinosaurs. Use this opportunity to review how the students can use the computer catalog to look up "dinosaur."

ACTIVITIES FOR TEACHERS

Decoding

The students may need to review or decode some of these words from the story.

voice	stare	stared	rope	ropes
noise	build	building	knock	instead
wait	waiting	haven't	either	delighted
cover	covered	watch	watched	wonderful

Phonics

Review –oi words such as:

oil	boil	foil	soil	toil
noise	voice	choice	poise	point

Phonemic Awareness

Review how new words are created by changing final consonants in the following:

beak	bean	card	cart	bat	back
goat	goal	cat	can	fat	fan
mean	meal	moon	mood	toot	tooth
rain	raid	fit	fish	fit	fin

Comprehension

Recall

Where did Danny go? *To a museum.*

What had the policeman never seen before? *A dinosaur stop for a red light.*

Why did the dog bark at the dinosaur? *He thought it was a car.*

How did the dinosaur help the lady with her bundles? *He carried her across the street.*

What did the dinosaur eat instead of grass? *Ice cream.*

Why did the man at the zoo want the dinosaur to leave the zoo? *Nobody was paying any attention to the other animals.*

Inferring

Why didn't the game of Hide and Seek work out very well? *The dinosaur could not hide because he was too big.*

Why did the children pretend not to see the dinosaur when he hid the second time? *Because they wanted him to have fun, too.*

Synthesizing

Suppose you could have a dinosaur friend for a day. What would you do?

WRITING ACTIVITIES

Main Idea

Write the main idea of the story in one sentence.

_____

_____

_____

Sequencing

Number the following events in the order they happened in the story.

_____ The dinosaur eats some ice cream.

_____ The dinosaur goes back to the museum.

_____ Danny goes to the museum to see what is inside.

_____ A dinosaur starts talking to Danny.

_____ The dinosaur does tricks for Danny and his friends.

Story Elements

Who are the main characters? _____

Where does the story take place? _____

What is the problem? _____

How is the problem solved? _____

Compare and Contrast

Compare the policeman with the zookeeper. How are they alike? How are they different?

_____

_____

_____

Summarizing

Write a summary of the story on another piece of paper.

PARENTS' PAGE

Dear Parents,

We have just finished reading the book *Danny and the Dinosaur* by Syd Hoff. Danny loves dinosaurs! So when one at the museum speaks to him, he is very excited. Danny and the dinosaur embark on a wonderful journey around town. They walk through the city with Danny riding on the dinosaur's back. They amaze a police officer, a dog, and the people in the buildings and on the street. The dinosaur is helpful, too. He becomes a bridge, a bus, and a boat when necessary. He is the most popular attraction at the zoo, much to the dismay of all the other animals. He is the best playmate Danny has ever had, and Danny wants to keep him. But the dinosaur says he has to go back to the museum. Danny decides this is for the best because there's no room at his house for a dinosaur anyway. The following activities will enhance your child's learning experience.

Enrichment Activities

Use clay and make models of various kinds of dinosaurs. Using a box tipped on its side as a background, you can make a diorama to show the environment of the dinosaurs.

Kits are available to build models that look like the dinosaur skeletons displayed at museums.

A trip to the museum to see prehistoric creatures would be a great experience.

Many children are fascinated with dinosaurs and prehistoric animals. There are many books on the subject. Here are a few:

Nonfiction

My Visit to the Dinosaurs by Aliki

What Happened to the Dinosaurs by Franklyn M. Branley

How Dinosaurs Came to Be by Patricia Lauber and Douglas Henderson

Raptors! The Nastiest Dinosaurs by Don Lessem and David Peters

Dinosaurs by Stephanie Turnbull and Uwe Mayer

Dinosaur Discoveries by Robin West

A Dinosaur Named Sue. The Story of the Colossal Fossil: The World's Most Complete T. Rex by Patricia Relf and Portia Sloan

Bigger Than T. Rex. The Discovery of Giganotosaurus: The Biggest Meat-Eating Dinosaur Ever Found by Don Lessem and Robert F. Walters

Fiction

What Happened to Patrick's Dinosaurs by Carol and Donald Carrick

Can I Have a Stegosaurus, Mom? Can I? Please? by Lois G. Grambling and H. B. Lewis

Five Silly Fisherman

by Roberta Edwards
Reading Level 1.5

Setting: Near a river in the country

Characters: Five fishermen

Plot: The five fishermen spend a nice day fishing at the river, but when it is time to go home, one of them seems to be missing.

Solution: It takes a little girl who has come to the lake to fish to straighten out a silly mistake the fishermen made.

Summary: The five fishermen go down to the river to fish. They each pick out their favorite spot and then warn the fish that they are going to catch them. At the end of the day, each fisherman has a nice, fat fish. When they get ready to leave, they decide to make sure everybody is safe and accounted for, but when they count heads, one fisherman is always missing, no matter who does the counting. A little girl figures out their problem and tricks them into giving her their fish by saying they must give them to her if she can find the missing fisherman. But she knows no one is really missing at all: each time one of the silly fishermen did the counting, he forgot to count himself!

Curriculum Connections: This is a good book to use with a math unit. There are five fishermen to start, but mental addition and subtraction can be practiced. For example, if two fishermen fall in the river, how many are left on the bank? One climbs out. Now how many are on the bank?

ACTIVITIES FOR MEDIA SPECIALISTS

Schema

Ask the students who has ever been fishing. Let them tell about their fishing experiences.

Predicting

Show the children the cover of the book. Have someone read the title. Ask what they think the title means, whether it is going to be a true story, and how they know.

Visualizing

Have children do the following exercise: Think of a place where you might go fishing. Make a picture in your mind. How many of you see a quiet place? How many see a noisy place? How many see a cold place? How many of you see a hot place? How many see yourselves on a boat? How many are on a river? A lake? An ocean?

Library Skills

On several fish-shaped cards, write names of places and things in the library. Using the game Go Fish, have the students fish for a card. When a student catches a fish, have him or her show the group what that word means in the library. The following words may be used:

computer	checkout desk	book cover
picture books	magazines	bookends
encyclopedias	nonfiction book	videos

ACTIVITIES FOR TEACHERS

Decoding

The students may need to review or decode some of the following words from the story:

climbed	ready	catch	each
count	another	wrong	drowned
mistake	splash	shouted	

Phonics

Review the sight words with students:

one	who	what	went	are
there	have	said	was	why

Phonemic Awareness

Focus on final phonemes. Use picture cards and turn them down in the middle of the group. Have the students choose a card. When they say the name of the picture, have them repeat the ending phoneme several times. For example, fish-sh-sh-sh-sh.

Comprehension

Recall

Name the places that each fisherman picked as his fishing spot. *rock, dock, tree, grass, boat*

What were they going to do with the fish? *Eat them for supper.*

Why did the fishermen cry and cry? *They thought they had lost their friend.*

What mistake did the five fishermen make while counting? *They didn't count themselves.*

Inferring

Why did the little girl ask the fishermen to jump into the river? *To count accurately.*

What was more important to the fishermen, the fish or their friend? How do you know? *Their friend, or accept any reasonable answer.*

Why were the fishermen so silly? *They did not count themselves.*

Synthesizing

The fish, birds, rabbits, and frog in the pictures are very interesting. Write a story about these animals and their thoughts about the fishermen.

Create a diorama in a shoebox with fish in the pond and the fishermen. You can use popsicle sticks for the fishermen and make clothes out of paper and use blue paper for a pond.

WRITING ACTIVITIES

Main Idea

Write the main idea of the story in one sentence.

_____

_____

_____

Sequencing

Number the following events in the order they happened in the story.

_____ A little girl comes by to go fishing, too.

_____ Five silly fishermen go fishing.

_____ The little girl sees the mistake right away.

_____ At the end of the day, each fisherman had a nice, fat fish on his line.

_____ They count to make sure no one is missing.

Story Elements

Who are the main characters? _____

Where does the story take place? _____

What is the problem? _____

How is the problem solved? _____

Compare and Contrast

Compare the five silly fishermen to the little girl. How are they alike? How are they different?

_____

_____

_____

Summarizing

Write a summary of the story on another piece of paper.

PARENTS' PAGE

Dear Parents,

We have just finished reading a book called *Five Silly Fishermen.* The five fishermen go down to the river to fish. They each pick out their favorite spot and then warn the fish that they are going to catch them. At the end of the day, each fisherman has a nice, fat fish. When they get ready to leave, they decide to make sure everybody is safe and accounted for, but when they count heads, one fisherman is always missing, no matter who does the counting. A little girl figures out their problem and tricks them into giving her their fish by saying the must give them to her if she can find the missing fisherman. But she knows no is really missing at all: each time one of the silly fishermen did the counting, he forgot to count himself!

This is a very funny story, and there are many sight words for the children to review (sight words are those that students must learn by memorizing them because the phonics rules do not apply). We have done some activities to review sight words, and this activity will help as well: have your child make a Go Fish game by writing sight words from the book on the cards (or any other words with which they may need help). They could make another game with library-related words on the cards.

The following activities provide additional ways to enhance your child's learning experience.

Enrichment Activities

To expand on the fish theme, it would be fun to take a trip to an aquarium or a retail fish or pet store.

If there is a family member interested in fishing, this would be a great time to expose your child to fishing if he or she has not already experienced it.

Talk about the difference between a creek, a stream, a river, and an ocean. If you live near any of these bodies of water, take a nature walk and check out the plants and animals. Collect specimens and make a scrapbook.

The following books may be interesting as a follow-up to this story:

Swimmy by Leo Lionni

The Rainbow Fish by Marcus Pfister

The Rainbow Fish and the Big Blue Whale by Marcus Pfister

The Rainbow Fish to the Rescue! by Marcus Pfister

Have your student write a story about or draw a picture of a beautiful, imaginary fish.

The Golly Sisters Go West

by Betsy Byars
Reading Level 2.1

Setting: On the trail heading out west

Characters: May-May and Rose Golly

Plot: The Golly sisters are heading west, and along the way they sing and dance to entertain people. They also fuss a great deal at each other. They still manage to have some interesting adventures and make the best of bad situations.

Solution: The Golly sisters finally figure out that they will get along better and not have so many troubles if they stop fussing at each other.

Summary: The Golly sisters are ready to go west, but the horse pulling the wagon just won't move. They finally remember that they must use "horse language," such as *giddy-up* and *whoa*. In the second chapter, the sisters get ready to put on a show, but they start arguing about who should go first. By the time they settle the argument, the audience is gone. In the third chapter, the sisters get lost, so they start singing as the horse continues to pull the wagon. Then they hear people clapping and realize they have reached a town. The sisters even try to get their horse to act in a show but find out the horse cannot dance. They have to change their act in the fifth chapter, when a red hat is squashed because of their fighting. Finally, they decide to stop fussing.

Curriculum Connections: Westward Expansion unit, humorous stories unit

---

ACTIVITIES FOR MEDIA SPECIALISTS

Schema

Find out what the children already know about wagon trains and why people were willing to move out West. Show some pictures from nonfiction books with actual wagons and wagon trains.

Predicting

After presenting the title, ask the students if they think "Golly Sisters" is a real name. Show them the picture on the cover of the book. What kind of a story do they think this is going to be?

Visualizing

Measure off a space on the floor equivalent to what it would be like inside a wagon so students can feel how cramped it might have been. Have children do the following exercise: Picture yourself riding in a covered wagon. What would it be like? How much room would you have to sleep?

Library Skills

Ask the students how they might find more humorous books. What keywords could they use to find them in the catalog?

ACTIVITIES FOR TEACHERS

Decoding

The students may need to review or decode some of these words from the story:

remembered	reins	curtain	admit
wonderful	worried	afraid	fussed

Phonics

Have the students make new words by adding a beginning sound to "est" and "ent."

west	test	pest	best	rest	vest	zest	crest
went	tent	dent	bent	rent	vent	spent	

Phonemic Awareness

Have the students learn the following poem.

The Golly Sisters Go West,

It turned out to be a big test,

They each thought the other a pest,

But finally decided to give it a rest.

Comprehension

Recall

Why wouldn't the horse go when the sisters said, "Go"? *They needed to use horse language such as* giddy-up *and* whoa.

Who was in the audience when May-May and Rose gave their very first show? *Dogs.*

How did making tea and singing help the sisters find their way? *It calmed them, and people could hear them.*

Inferring

Why do you think the sisters fussed so much? *Sisters just do that, because each wants her own way.*

How do you think the red hat got under the bed? *Accept any reasonable answer.*

Synthesizing

Think of a way May-May and Rose could have saved themselves a lot of trouble along the way west.

Perform a song or do a dance like the Golly Sisters might have done.

WRITING ACTIVITIES

Main Idea

Write the main idea of the story in one sentence.

_____

_____

_____

Sequencing

Number the following events in the order they happened in the story.

_____ May-May loses her hat.

_____ The Golly Sisters stop fussing.

_____ Rose and May-May give a show for dogs.

_____ The Golly Sisters get lost.

_____ The horse will not go.

Story Elements

Who are the main characters? _____

Where does the story take place? _____

What is the problem? _____

How is the problem solved? _____

Compare and Contrast

Compare Rose and May-May. How are they alike? How are they different?

_____

_____

Summarizing

Write a summary of the story on another piece of paper.

PARENTS' PAGE

Dear Parents,

We have just finished reading the book titled *The Golly Sisters Go West*. It is a very funny story. The Golly sisters are ready to go west, but the horse pulling the wagon just won't move. They finally remember that they must use "horse language" such as *giddy-up* and *whoa*. In the second chapter, the sisters get ready to put on a show, but they start arguing about who should go first. By the time they settle the argument, the audience is gone. In the third chapter, the sisters get lost, so they start singing as the horse keeps pulling the wagon. Then they hear clapping and realize they have reached a town. The sisters try to get their horse to act in a show but soon find out the horse cannot dance. They have to change their act in the fifth chapter when a red hat is squashed. Finally, they decide to stop fussing.

The following activities provide additional ways to enhance your child's learning experience.

Enrichment Activities

There are many museums that present the story of the Westward Expansion. Some even have real covered wagons.

The following books are good resources to learn more about the West and its stories.

Bandannas, Chaps, and Ten Gallon Hats by Bobbie Kalman

Red Flower Goes West by Ann W. Turner

Going West by Jean Van Leeuwen

Gold Fever by Verla Kay

Have your child write about what it might have been like to live in the Old West or draw a picture of him- or herself in a cowboy outfit.

The Great Snake Escape

by Molly Coxe
Reading Level 2.3

Setting: A park and zoo near a city

Characters: Mirabel the goose, Maxie the frog, and a king cobra snake

Plot: The king cobra snake has escaped from the park zoo, and Mirabel the goose and Maxie the frog want to find out what he eats because they do not want to be dinner for the snake.

Solution: After several adventurous ideas, the animal they fear the most helps them with their problem.

Summary: Mirabel the goose is on her way to visit her friend Maxie when she spies a newspaper article telling of an escaped snake from the zoo. Mirabel is afraid of snakes and hurries on to tell Maxie the frog about the zoo break. They both want to find out what king cobras eat because they do not want to become its dinner. They need to find the entire newspaper article so they check out the park. A gentleman is reading the paper, but he throws it away before they can read the whole article. Maxie and Mirabel know their lives are in danger if they cannot figure out what the snake eats, so they try to get the paper out of the trash. This is a difficult task for a goose and frog, however. Finally, Maxie decides he must jump into the trash container to read the newspaper article, but then he cannot get out. After several tries, Mirabel decides she must go home and get some string to pull Maxie from the trash. When she reaches home, she meets the king cobra snake that escaped from the zoo. He is very willing to help Mirabel and Maxie but does ask a small favor in return.

Curriculum Connections: Animal unit; character education—friendship unit: discuss how Mirable stuck by Maxie even though she was afraid of the snake.

ACTIVITIES FOR MEDIA SPECIALISTS

Schema

Ask the children what they know about zoos. Do they think the animals could escape easily? Have they ever heard of an animal escaping from a zoo? What would happen if an animal did escape?

Predicting

Show children the cover of the book and tell them to look especially at the face of the goose. Ask: What do you think she is looking for? Why?

Visualizing

Have the children visualize the following exercise: Picture yourself trapped in a cage or big trash bin. How would you feel? What would you do?

Library Skills

Present the term *newspaper*. Discuss why libraries keep newspapers and the purpose of a daily paper. Show the students the children's page from the newspaper.

ACTIVITIES FOR TEACHERS

Decoding

The students may need to review or decode some of the following words from the story:

newspaper	hopped	reading	headline
wrong	striped	tossed	lifted
wiggled	anywhere	garbage	slither
harbor	gangplank		

Phonics

Have the students add various beginning sounds to "ake," either on the board or on paper.

cake	bake	rake	fake
lake	make	sake	take
wake	flake	snake	brake
stake	shake	drake	Jake

Phonemic Awareness

Using the words from the phonics section and have the students make simple rhymes such as the following:

I saw a snake, I wanted to bake, I had to wake,
Making a shake. So I made a cake so I could bake.

Comprehension

Recall

How did Mirabel know that a snake had escaped from the zoo? *She read it in a newspaper that was on the ground.*

What was the man on the park bench reading about? *Baseball.*

What does a king cobra snake eat? *Other snakes and lizards.*

What were they going to do after they read what the snake ate? *Go swimming.*

Why did they have to hurry to get Maxie out of the trash can? *The garbage truck was coming.*

Inferring

Why do you think Mirabel could not push over the trash can? It doesn't look very heavy. *It is locked down in some way.*

Why would that be? *So the trash can would stay put and people would use it instead of littering.*

Synthesizing

Create a story about the king cobra and his trip on the ship to India.

WRITING ACTIVITIES

Main Idea

Write the main idea of the story in one sentence.

_____

_____

_____

Sequencing

Number the following events in the order they happened in the story.

_____ Mirabel meets the king cobra.

_____ Mirabel finds a newspaper.

_____ The snake lifts Maxie out of the trash can.

_____ The man with the newspaper throws it in the trash.

_____ Maxie gets stuck in the trash can.

Story Elements

Who are the main characters? _____

Where does the story take place? _____

What is the problem? _____

How is the problem solved? _____

Compare and Contrast

Compare Maxie and the king cobra snake. How are they alike? How are they different?

_____

_____

_____

Summarizing

Write a summary of the story on another piece of paper.

PARENTS' PAGE

Dear Parents,

We have just finished reading a very good story titled *The Great Snake Escape* by Molly Coxe. This is a story about a snake that has escaped from a zoo in the city. Mirabel the goose is on her way to visit her friend Maxie when she spies a newspaper article telling of the snake's escape. Mirabel is afraid of snakes and hurries on to tell Maxie the frog about the zoo break. They both want to find out what king cobras eat because they do not want to become its dinner. They need to find the entire newspaper article, so they check out the park. A gentleman is reading the paper, but he throws it away before they can read the whole article. Maxie and Mirabel know their lives are in danger if they cannot figure out what the snake eats, so they try to get the paper out of the trash. This is a difficult task for a goose and frog, however. Finally, Maxie decides he must jump into the trash container to read the newspaper article, but then he cannot get out. After several tries, Mirabel decides she must go home and get some string to pull Maxie from the trash. When she reaches home, she meets the king cobra snake that escaped from the zoo. He is very willing to help Mirabel and Maxie but does ask a small favor in return.

The following activities provide additional ways to enhance your child's learning experience.

Enrichment Activities

Some zoos have snake or reptile areas. Sometimes there are demonstrations showing how the snake is milked for its venom, which is then used to produce antivenom medications. You and your children may find it interesting to learn about the process.

There are also some places where children can actually hold a snake and are taught the differences between poisonous and nonpoisonous snakes and the good they do in the food chain by eating insects. There is a misconception that snakes are slimy feeling when in fact most of them are not.

There are some wonderful stories about snakes. For example:

Verdi by Janet Cannell

The Day Jimmy's Boa Ate the Wash by Trinka Hakes Noble

Hester by Jacqueline Sweeney

Hide and Snake by Keith Baker

Jake and the Snake by Kelli C. Foster

Have your child write about or draw a picture of a make-believe snake.

The Horse in Harry's Room

by Syd Hoff
Reading Level 2.3

Setting: Harry's room

Characters: Harry, his horse, and his mom and dad

Plot: Harry has a horse in his room, but no one else can see it. His parents want Harry to see a real horse so he understands that he could not possibly have a horse in his room.

Solution: Harry goes to the country and does see real horses. He then tells his horse that he can leave if he wants to run free, but his horse chooses to stay with Harry in his room. Harry now understands the difference between real and make-believe horses, but he still wants to keep his make-believe horse in his room.

Summary: Harry has a horse in his room that no one else can see. He rides and jumps the horse over objects without knocking over a thing. His parents hear him riding his horse, but they never see the animal. When Harry tells his classmates about his horse, they all laugh. Finally, his parents take Harry to the country to see real horses run, kick, and nibble so he will stop saying he has a horse in his room. When Harry returns from the country, he tells his horse that it can go and be free to run, kick, and nibble, but his horse does not want to go away. Now Harry knows his horse will always be there to watch over him.

Curriculum Connections: Fiction versus nonfiction, pet unit, imaginary friends

ACTIVITIES FOR MEDIA SPECIALISTS

Schema

Ask the children how many have ever had an imaginary friend. (They may not remember, but their parents may have told them about it.) Let them tell about their imaginary friends. Ask why they think little children have imaginary friends.

Predicting

Show the children the picture of the horse on the cover. Why do they think Harry's picture is in color and the horse is only a black outline drawing?

Do they think this is a happy story or a sad story? How can they tell?

Visualizing

Have students do the following exercise: Close your eyes and try to remember a time when you have seen horses. Where were they? What were they doing?

Library Skills

Ask children how they would find true (nonfiction) books about horses in the library. Review the use of keyword searches and call numbers to find the location of a subject.

ACTIVITIES FOR TEACHERS

Decoding

The students may need to review or decode the following words from the story:

nobody	knocking	ceiling
country	watch	dresser
chickens	nibbling	kicking

Phonics

Review the /oo/ vowel sound using the following words:

room	zoom	boom	doom
gloom	broom	groom	vroom
moon	soon	loon	noon

Phonemic Awareness

Review substitution of initial consonants with the /ight/ pattern.

light	fight	night	right
might	tight	sight	bright
blight	fright	plight	

Comprehension

Recall

Why did Harry's mother look into Harry's room? *To see what he was doing because she heard him talking to his horse.*

What did Harry say to make his horse go when he wanted to ride? *Giddyap!*

What did Harry say to make his horse stop? *Whoa!*

What did the teacher want the children to talk about? *Anything.*

Inferring

Do you think Harry liked seeing the real horses? *Accept any reasonable answer.*

Why did he go right to his room when he got home from the ride in the country? *He wanted to see if his horse wanted to go free.*

Why was it important for Harry's horse to stay? *Accept any reasonable answer about security and making Harry feel safe.*

Synthesizing

Make up a story about a little boy or girl who has an imaginary friend. It can be an animal or a person. What kinds of things do they do together? Compare your story to Harry's.

WRITING ACTIVITIES

Main Idea

Write the main idea of the story in one sentence.

_____

_____

_____

Sequencing

Number the following events in the order they happened in the story.

_____ Harry's mother and father take him for a ride in the country to see real horses.

_____ Harry's horse does not leave to run free, kick, and nibble.

_____ Harry's mother and father look into his room, but they do not see a horse.

_____ Harry has a horse in his room that nobody knows about.

_____ At school, Harry tells the class about the horse in his room.

Story Elements

Who are the main characters? _____

Where does the story take place? _____

What is the problem? _____

How is the problem solved? _____

Compare and Contrast

Compare Harry's horse to the horses in the field. How are they alike? How are they different?

_____

_____

_____

Summarizing

Write a summary of the story on another piece of paper.

PARENTS' PAGE

Dear Parents,

We have just finished reading the book *The Horse in Harry's Room* by Syd Hoff.

Harry has a horse in his room that no one else can see. He rides and jumps the horse over objects without knocking over a thing. His parents hear him riding his horse, but they never see the animal. When Harry tells his classmates about his horse, they all laugh. Finally, his parents take Harry to the country to see real horses run, kick, and nibble so he will stop saying he has a horse in his room. When Harry returns from the country, he tells his horse that it can go and be free to run, kick, and nibble, but his horse does not want to go away. Now Harry knows his horse will always be there to watch over him.

The following activities provide additional ways to enhance your child's learning experience.

Enrichment Activities

There are many opportunities to see horses. A drive in the country like the one Harry and his parents take would be a good way to observe horses. It might be possible to visit a stable where horses are kept for people who live in the city and do not have room for them.

There are also stables where children can learn to ride or go on trail rides. Vacation areas often have trail rides available as an activity.

This is a good book to begin a discussion about how to feel secure and safe. You might find out some interesting things about how your child feels.

The following books may be of interest to your child:

Nonfiction

The Checkerboard series by Janet L. Gammie includes the following titles: *Arabian Horses, Pinto Horses, Clydesdale Horses, Thoroughbred Horses,* and *Palomino Horses*

Horse Heroes: True Stories of Amazing Horses by Kate Petty

Fiction

Barney's Horse by Syd Hoff

Chester by Syd Hoff

Ice-Cold Birthday

by Maryann Cocca-Lefler
Reading Level 1.6

Setting: A seven-year-old girl's home

Characters: A seven-year-old girl, her mom, her dad, and her sister

Plot: The family plans a birthday party, but a huge snowstorm keeps all the kids at home.

Solution: Mom, Dad, and Sis help make the birthday fun even without lights or a baked birthday cake.

Summary: A seven-year-old girl is looking forward to her birthday party because she thinks it will change her luck—it's been all bad lately. The day of the party starts out well. It is snowing lightly, and it's beautiful outside. The weather takes a turn for the worse, however, and it is snowing very, very hard by the end of the school day. The radio announces heavy snow and high winds. The lights go out, and then the phone calls start coming. No one can come to the party. The little girl is miserable, but her family manages to save the day with ice cream cake with candles, a flashlight for shadow puppets, and a brand new sled. They have a great time, and the little girl decides she has good luck after all.

Curriculum Connections: Friendship unit, weather unit, making the best of a bad situation

ACTIVITIES FOR MEDIA SPECIALISTS

Schema

Ask the children to raise their hands if they have ever had a birthday party. Then ask if anyone has ever had a birthday party when something went wrong. (Have several tell their stories.)

Predicting

Tell the children that the title of the book is *Ice-Cold Birthday,* but do not show them the cover. Ask, "What do you think the title means?"

Visualizing

Have students do the following exercise: Close your eyes and picture in your head a birthday party in your honor. What is it like? How do you think the people feel? Where are you? Does anything unusual happen?

Library Skills

Show cards with call numbers on them. Check to see if the students know the difference between "E" books and "FIC" books and books with the Dewey Decimal numbers on them.

ACTIVITIES FOR TEACHERS

Decoding

The students may need to review or decode some of these words in the story.

people	parade	pancake	blowing
power	stared	shadow	spooky
admit	blindfolds	surprise	

Phonics

Review words with the "old" sound. Have the students make new words.

| cold | bold | fold | gold |
| hold | mold | sold | told |

Phonemic Awareness

Choose sentences from the story that have three, four, and five words in them. Read them aloud and have the students clap out how many words are in each sentence.

Comprehension

Recall

What happened on the Fourth of July when the girl carried the flag? *It rained.*
How many friends were coming to the birthday party? *Six.*

What started happening when the lights went out? *Friends begin to call the little girl saying they can't come to the party.*

What games did the family play? *Shadow puppets and pin-the-tail-on-the-donkey.*

What did the girl get for her birthday? *A sled.*

What was the best card she had ever gotten? *The big happy birthday in the snow.*

Inferring

Why did the girl feel lucky at the end of the story? *The snow made it a special birthday.*

Do you think Mom and Dad were having fun? Why or why not?

Why would Mom have to use the ice cream right away? *It would melt because the electricity went out.*

Synthesizing

Have students do the following:

Create an ice cream sculpture of your favorite animal.

Write or draw about one of your special birthdays.

WRITING ACTIVITIES

Main Idea

Write the main idea of the story in one sentence.

_____

_____

_____

Sequencing

Number the following events in the order they happened in the story.

_____ The radio says a bad storm is coming.

_____ The little girl gets a sled for her birthday.

_____ It starts snowing on the little girl's birthday.

_____ The lights go out.

_____ Mom bakes a big birthday cake.

Story Elements

Who are the main characters? _____

Where does the story take place? _____

What is the problem? _____

How is the problem solved? _____

Compare and Contrast

Compare a birthday party you have had with the one the little girl had. How are they alike? How are they different?

_____

_____

_____

Summarizing

Write a summary of the story on another piece of paper.

PARENTS' PAGE

Dear Parents,

We have just finished reading a book titled *Ice-Cold Birthday* by Maryann Cocca-Lefflert. A seven-year-old girl is looking forward to her birthday party because she thinks it will change her luck—it's been all bad lately. The day of the party starts out well. It is snowing lightly, and it's beautiful outside. The weather takes a turn for the worse, however, and it is snowing very, very hard by the end of the school day. The radio announces heavy snow and high winds. The lights go out, and then the phone calls start coming. No one can come to the party. The little girl is miserable, but her family manages to save the day with ice cream cake with candles, a flashlight for shadow puppets, and a brand new sled. They have a great time, and the little girl decides she has good luck after all.

The following activities provide additional ways to enhance your child's learning experience.

Enrichment Activities

This is a great story to discuss how to turn a bad situation into a good one. Discuss the old saying, "When life hands you a lemon, make lemonade." This is what this family accomplishes quite well. Give examples of your own "bad luck" and how you turned things around. Young children like hearing about adult real-life adventures.

Disappointment is a part of life. Discuss how we do get over our little disappointments.

If the weather is of interest to your child, the following books would be excellent resources for further reading:

The Big Snow by Berta and Elmer Hader

Snow Family by Daniel Kirk

The Snowy Day by Ezra Jack Keats

The Cloud Book by Tomie dePaola

Cloudy with a Chance of Meatballs by Judi Barrett

Have your student draw a picture or write about a favorite part of the story.

Little Bear

by Else Holmelund Minarik
Reading Level 2.4

Setting: Little Bear's Home

Characters: Little Bear and his mother

Plot: Little Bear and his mother have a lot of fun together, and Little Bear's imagination keeps them very busy.

Solution: Wise Mother Bear lets Little Bear play out his games.

Summary: There are four chapters in this book. The first chapter is "What Will Little Bear Wear?" Little Bear thinks he needs lots of warm clothes to play in the snow so Mother Bear bundles him up, but Little Bear finds out he already has a nice warm coat. In the second chapter, "Birthday Soup," Little Bear thinks his mother is gone and that there will be no food for the guests, so he makes soup. But Mother Bear is just out getting the cake. Chapter Three is called "Little Bear Goes to the Moon"—at least he thinks he does, until it's time for lunch. The last chapter is "Little Bear's Wish." His imagination is very busy, but Mother Bear knows he cannot have all the things he wishes for. When he wishes for stories, however, Mother Bear is very happy to tell him all about his very interesting day.

ACTIVITIES FOR MEDIA SPECIALISTS

Schema

Ask the students the following questions: How many of you have ever seen a bear? Where did you see the bear? How many have ever seen a mother bear and her baby? Do the babies stay close to their mothers? Why do you think that is?

Predicting

Ask the students the following questions: What would a mother bear and her cub do together in real life? Do you think they have fun together? How would a mother and her cub have fun together?

Visualizing

Have the students think about times they have made up games and then picture themselves playing these games. Ask several students to tell about the picture in their minds.

Library Skills

Ask the students the following questions:

Is this book fiction or nonfiction? How do you know?

What would you do if you wanted a true or nonfiction book about bears?

What keyword would you type into the computer?

How would you know by looking at the call numbers if the book is nonfiction?

What do we call the system that numbers the book by subject?

ACTIVITIES FOR TEACHERS

Decoding

The students may need to review or decode the following words from the story:

something	hurray	again	birthday
goodness	carrots	potatoes	peas
tomatoes	really	wait	beautiful
helmet	feathers	tumbled	Viking
China	would		

Phonics

Practice the /ake/ word family. Make new words beginning with the word *cake*.

bake	fake	lake
make	rake	snake
take	brake	flake

Phonemic Awareness

Practice seeing the difference between long words and short words. On the chalkboard or a poster, write the following words and discuss the length of each.

for	chop	some
forget	chopsticks	something
day	water	can
birthday	waterfall	cannot

COMPREHENSION

Recall

What three things did Mother Bear give Little Bear to keep him warm? *A hat, a coat, and snow pants.*

What four kinds of food did Little Bear put into the birthday soup? *Carrots, potatoes, peas, tomatoes.*

What happened to Little Bear when he tried to fly? *He came down with a plop.*

What were some of the things that Little Bear wished for? *To sit on a cloud, to sail with the Vikings, to tunnel to China, to have a big red car, and to visit a castle with a princess.*

Inferring

Why did Little Bear think there would be no birthday cake? *Because Mother Bear was not at home baking.*

Why do you think Mother Bear let Little Bear try to fly even though she knew he couldn't? *Sometimes you just have to let children make mistakes in order to learn.*

Synthesizing

Have students create their own space helmets with any materials that work for your class. Remind them not to jump out of any trees—they are not bears!

WRITING ACTIVITIES

Main Idea

Write the main idea of the story in one sentence.

_____

_____

_____

Sequencing

Number the following events in the order they happened in the story.

_____ Little Bear wears his own fur coat because he is cold.

_____ Little Bear sees that it is snowing.

_____ Little Bear puts on snow pants because he is cold.

_____ Little Bear puts on a coat because he is cold.

_____ Little Bear puts on a hat because he is cold.

Story Elements

Who are the main characters? _____

Where does the story take place? _____

What is the problem? _____

How is the problem solved? _____

Compare and Contrast

Compare the cat, the duck, and the chicken—the guests featured in Chapter Two. How are they alike? How are they different?

_____

_____

_____

Summarizing

Write a summary of the story on another piece of paper.

PARENTS' PAGE

Dear Parents,

We have just finished reading a book called *Little Bear.* There are four chapters in this book. The first is "What Will Little Bear Wear?" Little Bear thinks he needs lots of warm clothes to play in the snow so Mother Bear bundles him up, but Little Bear finds out he already has a nice warm coat. In the second chapter, "Birthday Soup," Little Bear thinks his mother is gone and that there will be no food for the guests, so he makes soup. But Mother Bear is just out getting the cake. Chapter Three is called "Little Bear Goes to the Moon"—at least he thinks he does, until it's time for lunch. The last chapter is "Little Bear's Wish." His imagination is very busy, but Mother Bear knows he cannot have all the things he wishes for. When he wishes for stories, however, Mother Bear is very happy to tell him all about his very interesting day.

Along with reading the story, we reviewed some library skills. We talked about some of the new words in the story and on the /ake/ word family. We answered comprehension questions about the story. The following activities will enrich the work your child has done at school.

Enrichment Activities

This would be a good time to visit a zoo and observe the bears, especially if there are baby bears.

Mother Bear and Little Bear have a wonderful relationship in the book. A discussion about how to respect members of the family and their individual differences and the need for independence would be an appropriate spin-off topic from this book.

Have your child write a story about or draw a picture of a bear he or she would like to have as a friend.

Have your child visit the library and check out some of the following books:

Fiction

Every Autumn Comes the Bear by Jim Arnosky
Snow Bear by Jean Craighead George
Young Larry by Daniel Pinkwater

Nonfiction

How Do Bears Sleep? by E. J. Bird
Polar Bears by Gail Gibbons
The Bear by Sabrina Crewe

Little Bear's Visit

by Else Holmelund Minarik
Reading Level 2.3

Setting: The home of Little Bear's Grandmother and Grandfather in the woods.

Characters: Little Bear, Grandmother Bear, Grandfather Bear, Mother Bear, and Father Bear

Plot: Little Bear is visiting Grandmother and Grandfather for the day, and his parents tell him not to make them too tired. They have a wonderful time telling stories and teasing each other. Grandfather Bear does have to take a little nap, but Little Bear refuses to admit he's tired. He tries very, very hard to stay awake until his parents come to pick him up, but it is very difficult.

Solution: Little Bear falls asleep while Grandfather Bear is still teasing him about how they never get tired when they are having so much fun.

Summary: In this chapter book, Little Bear visits his Grandmother and Grandfather. Little Bear loves to visit and see all the fun things in Grandmother and Grandfather's house. Little Bear loves to hear stories, and because Grandfather fell asleep in his chair, he begs Grandmother to tell him the story of his mother and the robin. Chapter Two is the story of how Mother Bear took in a little robin who could not find his nest, but eventually the robin becomes sad, and she lets him go free. Chapter Three is a story that Grandfather tells about a goblin that is frightened right out of his shoes. In Chapter Four, Little Bear insists that he is not tired, but he falls asleep before Mother Bear and Father Bear even leave Grandparents' house.

ACTIVITIES FOR MEDIA SPECIALISTS

Schema

Ask the children to talk about some of their experiences with their grandparents.

Predicting

Read the titles of each of the chapters. Ask the children what they think the chapters are going to be about.

Visualizing

Have the children picture in their mind a fun time they have had with their grandparents.

Library Skills

Tell the students that the pictures in this book were done by Maurice Sendak, a famous illustrator. Ask: What does the word *illustrator* mean?

Show the students other books illustrated by Maurice Sendak. They will likely be familiar with some of the books. Ask: Do you think there are other good stories in the library about grandparents? How would we be able to find out?

ACTIVITIES FOR TEACHERS

Decoding

The students may need to review or decode some of these words in the story.

tired	laughed	found
nicely	garden	oriole
world	hurrah	scared
closer	quiet	because

Phonics

Little Bear gave Grandmother and Grandfather big hugs. Ask the children to make new words that have the /ug/ ending.

hug	jug	mug
bug	dug	tug
plug	snug	chug

Phonemic Awareness

Have the students listen for the syllables. Tell the children that the goblin in the story talks in a very strange way. If they can figure out what word he is trying to say, they will get a hug (Hershey makes a candy hug). Say the words in a monotone voice.

gar-den	Grand-mo-ther	Grand-fa-ther
blue-bird	sum-mer-time	um-brel-la
flow-er-pot	stor-y-time	sleep-y-head
tel-e-phone	tel-e-vi-sion	bi-cy-cle

Comprehension

Recall

What did Little Bear have to eat at Grandmother's and Grandfather's house? *Bread and jam, cake and cookies, milk and honey, and an apple*

Where did Little Bear find Grandmother after Grandfather fell asleep? *In the garden.*

Why did Mother Bear's eyes fill with tears in the robin story? *She knew the robin was unhappy.*

What was chasing the goblin? *His own shoes.*

Where did Little Bear fall asleep when he was trying so hard to stay awake? *On the sofa.*

Inferring

How do you know Little Bear was a very polite bear? *He asked if he was eating too much.*

Do you think Grandfather was really scared when he told the goblin story? *No, he was teasing Little Bear.*

Why did Grandmother Bear call Little Bear a "scamp" in the last chapter? *He pretended to be asleep but really heard everything the adults were talking about.*

Synthesizing

Create your own story that you think Little Bear would like to hear.

WRITING ACTIVITIES

Main Idea

Write the main idea of the story in one sentence.

_____

_____

_____

Sequencing

Number the following events in the order they happened in the story.

_____ Grandfather Bear does a jig.

_____ Grandfather Bear falls asleep.

_____ Little Bear tried on Grandfather Bear's hat.

_____ Grandmother Bear told Little Bear a story.

_____ Little Bear went to visit Grandmother and Grandfather Bear.

Story Elements

Who are the main characters? _____

Where does the story take place? _____

What is the problem? _____

How is the problem solved? _____

Compare and Contrast

Compare Little Bear at the beginning of the story and at the end of the story. How is he the same? How is he different?

_____

_____

_____

Summarizing

Write a summary of the story on another piece of paper.

PARENTS' PAGE

Dear Parents,

We have just finished reading a book titled *Little Bear's Visit*. In this four-chapter book, Little Bear visits his grandparents. Little Bear loves to visit and see all the fun things in Grandmother and Grandfather's house. Little Bear loves to hear stories, and because Grandfather fell asleep in his chair, he begs Grandmother to tell him the story of his mother and the robin. Chapter Two is the story of how Mother Bear took in a little robin who could not find his nest, but eventually the robin becomes sad, and she lets him go free. Chapter Three is a story that Grandfather tells about a goblin that is frightened right out of his shoes. In Chapter Four, Little Bear insists that he is not tired, but he falls asleep before Mother Bear and Father Bear even leave Grandparents' house.

We have talked about some of the new words in the story and practiced the word family /ug/, as in "hug." We also worked on syllables. Ask your student to tell you what we did. This helps with memory and also reminds your student what we did in class. The following activities will also help to enrich this book for the student.

Enrichment Activities

This might be a good time to get out the picture album or videos taken of your child and his or her grandparents. Letting children talk about their memories and experiences is a wonderful way to help them build language and vocabulary.

If the grandparents are not nearby, students can write stories and draw pictures to send to them.

Grandfather in this book is a tease. If you have a family member or friend who is a tease, discuss this with your child. Some children do not know how to react to this kind of verbal fun.

If you have elderly neighbors, this might be a good time to pay them a visit. They probably have some interesting stories to tell.

Visit your library and find other books about grandparents or storytelling. Some of the following may be helpful.

Hooray for Grandparent's Day by Nancy Carlson

Dora's Book by Michelle Edwards

The Trees of the Dancing Goats by Patricia Polacco

The Keeping Quilt by Patricia Polacco

Have your student write or draw a picture of his or her Grandparents.

Mouse Tales

by Arnold Lobel
Reading Level 2.5

Setting: A little mouse house in the woods

Characters: Papa Mouse and seven little mice

Plot: The seven mice children all want a story before bedtime, so Papa Mouse says he will tell a story for each of them.

Summary: Each of the seven chapters in the book is a story that Papa Mouse tells. The seven little mice want a story before bedtime, so Papa Mouse decides to tell them one story for each mouse. The seven chapters in the book are each one of the stories he tells the little mice. The first chapter, "The Wishing Well," is about a well that is hurt when a little girl throws coins in it. "Clouds" is about a little mouse and his mother picking out shapes in the clouds. The "Very Tall Mouse and Very Small Mouse" see things very differently. Together "The Mouse and the Wind" create several problems that turn out to have a nice ending. "The Journey" is about a mouse trying to visit his mother who uses many interesting ways to get to her house. In the last chapter, "The Old Mouse," a mouse learns a good lesson about children.

Curriculum Connections: This book lends itself well to a storytelling unit. The stories are short and repetitive, so they are easy to learn. Each child may choose a different story or even make up one. The entire book could also be used as a play. Scripting it would not be difficult. Videotape the students telling the stories and/or acting out the play. Another idea is to use a paper pattern of a mouse with a long tail on which the students may write "mouse tales." Make a bulletin board with the title "Mouse Tales for Mouse Tails." Discuss homophones.

ACTIVITIES FOR MEDIA SPECIALISTS

Schema

Ask students the following questions:

Does anyone have a pet mouse? How do you care for it?

Has anyone ever thrown a coin and wished in a wishing well or fountain? Where do you suppose this custom began?

How many of you have ever sat and watched clouds and tried to find shapes?

One of the stories is about a journey. How many different ways might a person travel?

Visualizing

Ask the students to do the following exercise: One of the stories in the book is about the wind. Imagine you are on a sailboat. What do you see? What do you feel? What do you smell?

Library Skills

Use the book's table of contents to preview the chapters in the book and motivate the students to read. Point out the page numbers and demonstrate to the children how to turn to a specific chapter.

ACTIVITIES FOR TEACHERS

Decoding

The students may need to review or decode the following words from the story.

threw	pillow	castle	horrid
wish	wished	wishing	suspenders
pictures	nearer	together	chewing
cellar	puddles	ceiling	whole
mountain	island	brought	snoring

Phonics

Using the two word families of "–ale" and "–ail," have the students make new words. Discuss how some of the following pairs are homophones:

tale	male	pale	sale	stale	scale	whale	
tail	mail	pail	sail	nail	fail	frail	trail

Phonemic Awareness

Use the words from the decoding list and have the students clap their hands to show they understand how many syllables are in each word

Comprehension

Recall

How did the little girl in "The Wishing Well" solve the problem of the coins hurting? *She used a pillow.*

Why did the little mouse become afraid of the cloud shape? *It was a cat!*

Name some things that the very tall mouse saw. *Birds, flowers, roofs, raindrops, ceilings.*

Name some things that the very short mouse saw. *Bugs, roots, cellar, puddles, floor.*

What did they both see together? *They saw a rainbow.*

How many different winds helped the mouse when he called for help? *Four: The north, south, east, and west winds.*

What are the various ways that helped the mouse get to his mother? *He used a car, rollerskates, boots, sneakers, and his feet.*

What did the children give the old mouse to hold up his pants? *The gave him chewing gum.*

Why did the mouse in the last chapter keep the water running? *He was still dirty.*

Inferring

Why did the very tall mouse and the very small mouse get along even though they saw things very differently? *They respected each other.*

In the story about the journey, what is very silly? *Putting on new feet.*

Synthesizing

Continue the story of "The Very Tall Mouse and the Very Short Mouse" in the same pattern and tell more things they might see up high and down low.

WRITING ACTIVITIES

Main Idea

Write the main idea of the story in one sentence.

_____

_____

_____

Sequencing

Number the following events in the order they happened in the story.

_____ The Old Mouse

_____ The Bath

_____ Very Tall Mouse and Very Short Mouse

_____ The Mouse and the Winds

_____ The Journey

_____ Clouds

_____ The Wishing Well

Story Elements

Who are the main characters? _____

Where does the story take place? _____

What is the problem? _____

How is the problem solved? _____

Compare and Contrast

Compare Papa Mouse with "The Old Mouse." How are they alike? How are they different?

_____

_____

_____

Summarizing

Write a summary of the story on another piece of paper.

PARENTS' PAGE

Dear Parents,

We have just finished reading a book called *Mouse Tales*. Each of the seven chapters in the book is a story that Papa Mouse tells. The seven little mice want a story before bedtime, so Papa Mouse decides to tell them one story for each mouse. The seven chapters in the book are each one of the stories he tells the little mice. The first chapter, "The Wishing Well," is about a well that is hurt when a little girl throws coins in it. "Clouds" is about a little mouse and his mother picking out shapes in the clouds. The "Very Tall Mouse and Very Small Mouse" see things very differently. Together "The Mouse and the Wind" create several problems that turn out to have a nice ending. "The Journey" is about a mouse trying to visit his mother who uses many interesting ways to get to her house. In the last chapter, "The Old Mouse," a mouse learns a good lesson about children.

The following activities provide additional ways to enhance your child's learning experience.

Enrichment Activities

This book is great for storytelling activities. Let your student retell the stories in the book. They do not have to be repeated exactly as they were told in the book; simply let your student tell stories and talk. Verbalizing what they are thinking and what is happening in their lives helps them to cement their thoughts and opinions.

Tell stories to your children about when you were little. They love hearing what your life was like and that you had some of the same thoughts, problems, and experiences that they are going through.

If you do not feel comfortable telling stories, a relative or friend may be good at it.

Take your child to a storytelling program. Many public libraries have visiting storytellers.

The mice in the stories are imaginary, but there are good nonfiction books if your child is interested in these animals. The following is a list of more fictional books that you can read with your child.

> *The Mouse and the Motorcycle* by Beverly Cleary
>
> *Geraldine the Music Mouse* by Leo Lionni
>
> *Frederick* by Leo Lionni
>
> *Stuart Little* by E. B. White
>
> *A Mouse Called Wolf* by Dick King-Smith

Have your student write about or draw a picture of a favorite chapter in the book *Mouse Tales*.

The Mystery of the Pirate Ghost

by Geoffrey Hayes
Reading Level 2.8

Setting:	Boogle Bay
Characters:	Otto, Uncle Tooth, Auntie Hick, Captain Poopdeck, Joe Puffin, Widow Mole, Blackeye Doodle, Ducky Doodle
Plot:	Strange things are happening in Boogle Bay: people are seeing ghosts, things are disappearing, and dead pirates are appearing to haunt the towns-people. The residents of Boogle Bay are frightened, and they want answers!
Solution:	Otto and Uncle Tooth decide to solve the mystery by following the clues, which lead to a very surprising ending.
Summary:	One day, Otto and Uncle Tooth are cleaning out the attic. They find a trumpet, and Uncle Tooth tells Otto he may have it. Otto is very excited and plays the instrument as he walks around the village. On his walk, he learns about a number of robberies. He scares Auntie Hick, who was already jumpy—she believes she has just seen a ghost! Thus begins a series of events that are lead to an adventure for Otto and his friends in Boogle Bay. They believe the robberies done by the ghost of Blackeye Doodles, a pirate who drown at sea. As it turns out, Blackeye's orphan son, Ducky Doodles, is stealing things to survive. He ran away from the orphanage to become a pirate like his father. Otto and Uncle Tooth decide to help Ducky get a job and repay the folks from whom he stole things. Not only do they solve the mystery of the pirate ghost, now that they've had a taste of adventure, they decide to start a detective agency in search of more excitement.

Curriculum Connections: Writing mystery stories, rocks and cave unit

ACTIVITIES FOR MEDIA SPECIALISTS

Schema

Ask the students if they have ever lost something, and it became a real mystery as to what had happened. Tell them, "This has happened to us all. Our story today is even more exciting! It is a mystery about a pirate!" What other stories do they know with pirates in them?

Visualizing

Have students do the following exercise: Picture yourself near the ocean in a little village where pirates hang out. You hear there are strange things happening, and a long dead pirate is being blamed for them. How do you feel?

Library Skills

Discuss the elements of a mystery:

Suspense: emotions are touched and we want to keep reading

A hook: something to grab your interest at the beginning of the story

Danger: this can be in the form of risk, intrigue, violence

Foreshadowing: author leaves clues in the story as to the solution

Cliffhangers: a technique used at the end of chapters to keep us reading

Strong characters: usually very interesting, striking characters

ACTIVITIES FOR TEACHERS

Decoding

The students may need to review or decode the following words from the story.

trumpet	laundry	muttered	clothesline
ghost	screeching	tiptoed	special
lure	crouched	delicious	lantern
sword	breathe	bloodcurdling	orphanage

Phonics

Review the vowel/consonant/silent e pattern with words from the story.

cave	take	hide	pipe	note
gave	fade	life	aside	cove
came	strange	knife	crime	whole
made	face time	twice	stole	

Phonemic Awareness

Have the students clap out the syllables of the following compound words:

houseboat	clothesline	crossbones	gumdrops
saltwater	moonlight	doorway	midnight
fishnet	manhole	spyglass	bloodcurdling

Comprehension

Recall

Where did Uncle Tooth find the silver trumpet he used during his sailor days? *He found it on Foghorn Island.*

Where does captain Poopdeck live? *He lives on a houseboat.*

What did the ghost thief take from Auntie Hick's shop? *He took boxes of saltwater taffy and a deck of cards.*

Uncle Tooth had seen many strange things in his day but never what? *A note from a ghost.*

What was the name of the place where Widow Mole had her pool hall? *Deadman's Landing.*

Inferring

Why did Otto jump up and down when Auntie Hick said she had seen a ghost? *He wanted an adventure.*

What does a "skull and crossbones" stand for? *Pirates or poison.*

Why do you think the Pool Hall got very quiet when Otto and Uncle Tooth arrived? *They mentioned the word "ghost."*

Why do you think the ghost wanted the hat back so badly? *It was his father's hat.*

What clue helped Otto find the cave? *A playing card stuck to a bush.*

Synthesizing

Have students do the following: Create a mini-mystery. Hide something in the room. Write clues to help others find it. Start with the hardest clues and make them easier. Don't give the location away too easily.

WRITING ACTIVITIES

Main Idea

Write the main idea of the story in one sentence.

_____

_____

_____

Sequencing

Number the following events in the order they happened in the story.

_____ Blackeye Doodle's hat lands on an octopus.

_____ Auntie Hick's shop is robbed.

_____ Ducky Doodle goes to work for Auntie Hick.

_____ Otto and Uncle Tooth are cleaning the attic.

_____ Otto finds a little cave.

Story Elements

Who is the main character? _____

Where does the story take place? _____

What is the problem? _____

How is the problem solved? _____

Compare and Contrast

Compare Otto and Ducky Doodle. How are they alike? How are they different?

_____

_____

_____

Summarizing

Write a summary of the story on another piece of paper.

PARENTS' PAGE

Dear Parents,

We have just finished reading a story titled *The Mystery of the Pirate Ghost* by Geoffrey Hayes. The title alone is enough to get the attention of the students. Here is a summary of the story. One day, Otto and Uncle Tooth are cleaning out the attic. They find a trumpet, and Uncle Tooth tells Otto he may have it. Otto is very excited and plays the instrument as he walks around the village. On his walk, he learns about a number of robberies. He scares Auntie Hick, who was already jumpy—she believes she had just seen a ghost! Thus begins a series of events that lead to an adventure for Otto and his friends in Boogle Bay. They believe the robberies done by the ghost of Blackeye Doodles, a pirate who drown at sea. As it turns out, Blackeye's orphan son, Ducky Doodles, is stealing things to survive. He ran away from the orphanage to become a pirate like his father. Otto and Uncle Tooth decide to help Ducky get a job and repay the folks from whom he stole things. Not only do they solve the mystery of the pirate ghost, now that they've had a taste of adventure, they decide to start a detective agency in search of more excitement.

The following activities provide additional ways to enhance your child's learning experience.

Enrichment Activities

Cave tours are offered in many parts of the country. If your child has never been in a cave, it would be quite an experience. There are many different kinds of caves in various parts of the country, and it would be exciting to explore any of them on trips. The following Web sites may be of help in planning such a trip:

National Speleological Society: http://nss@caves.org

National Caves Association: http://cavern.com

The following nonfiction books may be of interest:

Caves and Caverns by Gail Gibbons

Caves (Read All about Earthly Oddities) by Patricia Armentrout

Cave (One Small Square) by Donald M. Silver

Some children love ghost stories, and others do not. Depending on your student's preference, you may want to check out some of these books:

The Legend of Sleepy Hollow by Washington Irving

The Teeny-Tiny Woman by Paul Galdone

The following are just fun ghost stories and not scary at all:

Babar and the Ghost by Laurent de Brunhoff

A Ghost Named Fred by Nathaniel Benchley

Pirate stories may be of interest after reading this book:

Tough Boris by Mem Fox

Edward and the Pirates by David McPhail

How I Became a Pirate by Melinda Long

No Fighting, No Biting!

by Else Holmelund Minarik
Reading Level 2.6

Setting: The home of Rosa and Willy and Cousin Joan

Characters: Rosa, Willy, and Cousin Joan

Plot: Cousin Joan really wants to read, but Rosa and Willy keep bothering each other and will not sit still and read. So Cousin Joan tries to settle them by telling a story.

Solution: Cousin Joan tells the children a story about alligators fighting and biting, which helps Rosa and Willy to realize that reading their books is a much more pleasant activity.

Summary: Cousin Joan is trying to read her book, and Rosa and Willy want to sit with her, but they keep squeezing and pinching each other. Cousin Joan is reading a book about alligators, so she tells them a story about big hungry alligator and about how alligators fight and bite each other. But even when she finishes the story, the children have more questions about the big hungry alligator, so Cousin Joan has to tell them another story. This time the mother alligator makes the little alligators promise to listen to her when she says, "No fighting, no biting." Cousin Joan hopes the story will teach Rosa and Willy a lesson, and finally it does.

Curriculum Connections: Storytelling unit, animal unit, character education—getting along

ACTIVITIES FOR MEDIA SPECIALISTS

Schema

Ask the children if they ever have trouble getting along with their brothers and sisters. Let a few children tell their story. Explain that siblings often do have arguments. Ask them to think about why that is.

Predicting

Show the students some of the pictures in the book and have them notice the facial expressions of all three characters. Ask why they think they look the way they do. What might be happening?

Visualizing

Have students do the following exercise: Imagine that you and a brother or sister or friend are not getting along. What would you do to solve the problem?

Library Skills

The illustrator of this book is famous. Show the children some other books that Maurice Sendak has illustrated. Ask what they think makes him a good illustrator.

ACTIVITIES FOR TEACHERS

Decoding

The following words in the story have /ed/ and /ing/ endings added. The students may need to review them.

squeeze	squeezing	whisper	whispered
pinch	pinched	fight	fighting
bite	biting	climb	climbed
hurry	hurried	roar	roared
laugh	laughed	wriggle	wriggled

Phonics

Change the beginning sound with the ending "–ight" to make the following words:

fight	right	light	might
sight	night	tight	flight
plight	bright	fright	slight

Phonemic Awareness

Have the students practice rhyming sounds using a bean bag or soft foam ball and standing in a circle. The teacher says a word and tosses the ball to another student, who must say a rhyming word. If they cannot think of a rhyming word, they sit down until they can help someone else.

Fluency

Use the following rhyme to develop fluency:

Mama said, "No fighting,"
Mama said, "No biting,"
Light-foot said, "I will stop."
Quick-foot said, "On the spot!"

Comprehension

Recall

Are baby alligators safe from big older alligators? *No, if older alligators are hungry, they will eat babies.*

What was one way the big alligator was trying to get the little ones in his mouth? *He said he would carry them over the log in his mouth. He tried to talk them into counting his teeth.*

Why is Cousin Joan holding her head in the pictures in the last chapter? *The children are fussing at each other again.*

Inferring

Why did the big alligator just go away when the mother alligator told him to? *It is a fact of nature that mother animals are fierce in protecting their young.*

Why didn't the little alligators just walk around the log? *Accept any reasonable answer.*

Synthesizing

How would you solve the problem of the two children fussing at each other? *Accept any reasonable answer.*

WRITING ACTIVITIES

Main Idea

Write the main idea of the story in one sentence.

_____

_____

_____

Sequencing

Number the following events in the order they happened in the story.

_____ Rosa loses her tooth.

_____ Rosa and Willy squeeze and pinch each other.

_____ Cousin Joan, Rosa, and Willy are all reading.

_____ Cousin Joan wants to read.

_____ Cousin Joan tells a story about two little alligators.

Story Elements

Who are the main characters? _____

Where does the story take place? _____

What is the problem? _____

How is the problem solved? _____

Compare and Contrast

Compare Rosa and Willy. How are they alike? How are they different?

_____

_____

_____

_____

Summary

Write a summary of the story on another piece of paper.

PARENTS' PAGE

Dear Parents,

We have just finished reading the book *No Fighting, No Biting* by Else Homelund Minarik. This reader has four chapters. Cousin Joan is trying to read her book, and Rosa and Willy want to sit with Cousin Joan, but they keep squeezing and pinching each other. Cousin Joan is reading a book about alligators, so she tells them a story about a big hungry alligator and about how alligators fight and bite each other. But even when she finishes the story, the children have more questions about the big hungry alligator, so Cousin Joan has to tell them another story. This time the mother alligator makes the little alligators promise to listen to her when she says, "No fighting, no biting." Cousin Joan hopes the story will teach Rosa and Willy a lesson, and finally it does.

The following activities provide additional ways to enhance your child's learning experience.

Enrichment Activities

Most siblings do pester each other from time to time. This would be a good story to read again and adapt to your situation if the children in your family have similar issues. It just might lead to a very productive discussion about how to treat each other. It might also be helpful to tell about your own issues with siblings when you were young.

The clothes worn by the characters in the book are quite different from the clothes children wear today. Talk about the early 1900s when this story might have taken place. Discuss other changes in apparel from other periods of history.

If your child is an animal lover, the alligator stories might spark an interest in finding out more about them. Many zoos have reptile houses where your child could get a good look at a live alligator. If this is not possible, there are many informative nonfiction books.

Nonfiction

Alligators by James E. Gerholdt

Alligators by Patricia Kendell

Alligators by Julie Murray

Alligators and Crocodiles by Gerald Legg

Fiction

Bill and Pete by Tomie dePaola

Bill and Pete Go Down the Nile by Tomie dePaola

Bill and Pete to the Rescue by Tomie dePaola

Zack's Alligator Goes to School by Shirley Mozelle

No Mail for Mitchell

by Catherine Siracusa
Reading Level 1.8

Setting: Delivery route and neighborhood of Mitchell the mailman

Characters: Mitchell the mailman, Mr. Pig, Mr. Owl, Mrs. Groundhog, Mrs. Mouse, and the Beaver Family

Plot: Mitchell loves delivering the mail, but sadly, his mailbox is always empty. He really wishes he would receive a letter. One day he has to deliver a special package to Bobby Beaver for his birthday. Unfortunately, there's a terrible rainstorm, and Mitchell catches a bad cold. Mitchell has to stay in bed for two days and cannot do his job. The people on his route miss him very much!

Solution: Mitchell receives a great deal of mail because everyone misses him so much!

Summary: Mitchell feels bad because he delivers mail to everyone else, but he never gets any mail in his mailbox. He finds out just how much he is appreciated when he comes down with a cold and misses work for a few days.

Curriculum Connections: Language arts—letter writing unit. This book would be an excellent introduction to a letter writing unit. The teacher can instruct the class on the mechanics of letter writing including the greeting, the body of the letter, and the salutation. Students could write letters to their parents and tell them what they have learned in a particular subject.

ACTIVITIES FOR MEDIA SPECIALISTS

Schema

Ask your students: How many have ever received a letter? Is it fun to get mail? Why is that? What kind of mail have you received? How do you get your mail? Post office box? Mailbox? Delivered by truck? Community mailboxes?

Visualizing

Ask your students to do the following exercise: The mail must be delivered no matter what the weather is. Close your eyes and picture the worst rainstorm you have ever been in. What does it feel like? Would you want to deliver the mail in that kind of weather?

Predicting

Tell your students to look at Mitchell's uniform in the picture on the cover of the book. Ask what they think he does for a living. Show the students the cover of the book. Ask students why they think Mitchell is looking so sad and forlorn.

Library Skills

Ask students: How could we find a true (nonfiction) book about the U.S. Postal Service?

ACTIVITIES FOR TEACHERS

Decoding

The students may need to review or decode the following words from the story:

delivers	package	magazine	through
phone	special	puddle	answers

Phonics

Practice the /ail/ word family. Make new words beginning with "mail."

mail	sail	tail	bail
main	rain	gain	pain
grain	chain	brain	stain

Phonemic Awareness

Make a word card for each word in the Phonics section above. Place the word cards on a table or in a pocket chart. Pronounce each word slowly, drawing out each phoneme. Have the students point or choose the correct word. Then have the children each say their word or words and have the other students pronounce the word as a whole.

Comprehension

Recall

Why does Mitchell write a letter to himself? *Because he never gets any mail.*

Who received a magazine? *Mrs. Mouse.*

Why did Mitchell have to go out in the rainstorm? *He had to deliver a special package to Bobby Beaver, and the mail must be delivered in all kinds of weather.*

What three things did Mitchell do while he was home in bed with a cold? *He drank tea with honey, he read books, and he watched TV.*

Inferring

Does Mitchell live in a big city or a small town? *He lives in a small town.* How do you know? *Everyone knows each other.*

Why do you think Mr. Pig says to Mitchell, "I can always count on you"? *He always delivers the mail, every day without fail.*

How do you think Mitchell feels when he has to call in sick? *Terrible.*

Why do you think Mr. Pig is willing to deliver the mail for Mitchell? *Because he is a good worker most of the time.*

What other animals might live in the town? *Accept any reasonable answer.*

What time of year is it? *It is wintertime.*

Even though Mitchell was very tired, he felt good when he went to bed. Why? *His friends showed how much they cared for him.*

Synthesizing

Draw a picture of your neighborhood. Pretend you are the mail carrier and plan your mail route.

Using blocks or Lincoln Logs, design a little community.

WRITING ACTIVITIES

Main Idea

Write the main idea of the story in one sentence.

_____

_____

_____

Sequencing

Number the following events in the order they happened in the story.

_____ Mr. Pig calls Mitchell with a special message.

_____ Mr. Pig delivers a big bag of mail for Mitchell.

_____ Mitchell wakes up with a bad cold.

_____ The wind blows away Mitchell's letter to himself.

_____ Mitchell delivers Bobby Beaver's present.

Story Elements

Who are the main characters? _____

Where does the story take place? _____

What is the problem? _____

How is the problem solved? _____

Compare and Contrast

Compare Mitchell and Mr. Pig. How are they alike? How are they different?

_____

_____

_____

_____

Summary

Write a summary of the story on another piece of paper.

PARENTS' PAGE

Dear Parents,

We have just finished reading *No Mail for Mitchell* by Catherine Siracusa. Poor Mitchell the dog is the mailman. He is a very conscientious worker and loves his job, but one thing bothers him: he never receives any mail. One day, he finds out how much he is appreciated when he becomes ill and has to miss work.

The following activities provide additional ways to enhance your child's learning experience.

Enrichment Activities

Visit a post office at a time when it is not busy. You might be able to get a tour.

Many people enjoy stamp collecting. This may be a good time to introduce collectibles to your student. There are many good history lessons in stamp collecting.

Visit your library and check out books about the post office and stamp collecting such as the following:

The Post Office Book: Mail and How It Moves by Gail Gibbons

Out and About at the Post Office by Kitty Shea

We Need Mail Carriers by Lola M. Schaefer

Would You Mail a Hippo? by Viki Woodworth

The Jolly Postman or Other People's Letters by Janet and Allan Ahlberg

Writing Practice

Encourage your children to do the following:

Write a letter to someone they have not seen for a while.

Write postcards to friends when your family takes a trip.

Write cards to people in a nursing home. Your child might consider adopting an elderly friend.

Write to a classmate.

No More Monsters for Me!

by Peggy Parish
Reading Level 1.7

Setting: The woods surrounding the home of Minneapolis Simpkin, a little girl who wants a pet very, very badly.

Characters: Minneapolis Simpkin, her mother, and a "monster"

Plot: Minneapolis really, really wants a pet. Her mother does not realize just how badly.

Solution: Minneapolis Simpkin finally gets a pet after her actions make her mother realize that she is not just playing a game.

Summary: Minneapolis Simpkin and her mother are yelling at each other much too often because Minn wants a pet, and her mother won't allow it. One night, Minn takes a walk because she is so upset with her mother. She hears something crying in the woods. It is a baby monster! She takes it home and hides it in the basement. He eats food that is stored in the basement and continues to get bigger and bigger. Mother hears a noise and tells Minn to close the window in the basement. Minn knows it is the monster, but Mother thinks Minn's interest in monsters and her odd behavior is just a game. Minneapolis gets so upset when she tells her mom she brought home a pet monster that she begins to bawl. Mom then realizes that Minn really does need a pet, and they make a deal: if Minn gets rid of the monster, Mother will let her get a real pet.

Curriculum Connections: Pet unit. Many children have pets, but some cannot because of family allergies, because they live somewhere that doesn't allow pets, or for other reasons. This would be a great book to use during a pet unit to help kids understand the many situations in which people live, the needs a pet will have, and the commitment someone must have to take care of a pet properly.

ACTIVITIES FOR MEDIA SPECIALISTS

Schema

Ask how many students have pets. Ask how many have dogs, cats, and so on. Be prepared for many hands in the air. The students will all want to talk at the same time and tell you about their beloved pets.

Predicting

Show the students the cover of the book. Ask them why they think you asked questions about pets since there is a strange looking character on the cover, rather than a dog or cat.

Visualizing

Ask students to do the following exercise: What would it be like if you had to hide your pet and could not let anybody else in the family know about it?

Library Skills

Ask students: Are there such things as monsters? Do you think we have books in the library about monsters? What kind of books would they be, fiction or nonfiction?

Next, go to the computer catalog and, using *monster* as the keyword, show the students the kind of books that you find.

ACTIVITIES FOR TEACHERS

Decoding

The students may need to review or decode the following words from the story.

listened	surprised	bawling	myself
thought	basement	pickles	awful
lumpy	wrong	bother	crawl

Phonics

Add the "–ed" ending to words.

start *started*	surprise *surprised*
yell *yelled*	stamp *stamped*
walk *walked*	stop *stopped*
look *looked*	need *needed*
ask *asked*	grab *grabbed*
laugh *laughed*	open *opened*

Phonemic Awareness

Ask students: How many sounds do you hear in the following words? Hold up your fingers to answer.

h-u-g (3)	y-e-ll (3)	o-p-e-n (4)	M-o-m (3)
p-e-t (3)	f-oo-d (3)	h-i-d (3)	n-ee-d (3)
p-u-p (3)	k-i-tt-e-n (5)	h-i-ll-s (4)	j-u-m-p (3)

Comprehension

Recall

What did the monster eat first? *Apples.*

What else did the monster eat? *Potatoes.*

What did Mom say when Minn asked her what monsters eat? *Pickles.*

What happened every time the monster ate something? *He grew bigger.*

Inferring

Why do you think Mom told Minn not to bother looking for the monster caves? *She didn't want her to go searching through caves in the woods. It might be dangerous.*

Do you think there was really a monster in the basement?

Do you think Mom thought there was a monster in the basement? Why or why not?

Why do you think Minn wanted a pet so badly?

Synthesizing

Design a home for a monster just in case a real one comes to visit.

WRITING ACTIVITIES

Main Idea

Write the main idea of the story in one sentence.

_____

_____

_____

Sequencing

Number the following events in the order they happened in the story.

_____ The monster and Minn make a deal.

_____ Mom is really mad at Minneapolis Simpkin.

_____ The monster eats all the potatoes.

_____ Minn finds a baby monster in the bushes.

_____ The monster eats all the apples.

Story Elements

Who are the main characters? _____

Where does the story take place? _____

What is the problem? _____

How is the problem solved? _____

Compare and Contrast

Compare Minneapolis Simpkim and yourself. How are you alike? How are you different?

_____

_____

_____

_____

Summarizing

Write a summary of the story on another piece of paper.

PARENTS' PAGE

Dear Parents,

We have just finished reading a story called *No More Monsters for Me* by Peggy Parish. The little girl in the story, Minneapolis Simpkin, and her mother are yelling at each other much too often because Minn wants a pet, and her mother won't allow it. One night, Minn takes a walk because she is so upset with her mother. She hears something crying in the woods. It is a baby monster! She takes it home and hides it in the basement. He eats food that is stored in the basement and continues to get bigger and bigger. Mother hears a noise and tells Minn to close the window in the basement. Minn knows it was the monster, but Mother thinks Minn's interest in monsters and her odd behavior is just a game. Minneapolis gets so upset when she tells her mom she brought home a pet monster that she begins to bawl. Mom then realizes that Minn really does need a pet, and they make a deal: if Minn gets rid of the monster, Mother will let her get a real pet.

The following activities provide additional ways to enhance your child's learning experience.

Enrichment Activities

Discuss monsters with your child. One definition of a monster in Webster's dictionary is "an animal of strange or terrifying shape; one unusually large of its kind." We refer to the Loch Ness Monster, Big Foot, Frankenstein, and large scary characters as monsters, but these are just stories. Some children love stories about monsters, and others do not. If your child is afraid or concerned about monsters or other scary creatures, now is a good time to talk about it and help him or her overcome any fears. There are many fun monsters, too, such as the ones in *Shrek, Monsters Inc.,* and *Beauty and the Beast.*

Have your child write a story about or draw a picture of a monster.

The following books will be of interest if your child would like to read more about monsters.

Fiction

100 Monsters in My School by Bonnie Bader

Brave Little Monster by Ken Baker

Folklore

The Barefoot Book of Monsters by Fran Parnell

Beastly Tales: Yeti, Bigfoot, Lock Ness Monster by Malcolm Yorke

Nonfiction

Animals Nobody Loves by Seymour Simon

Oliver

by Syd Hoff
Reading Level 2.1

Setting: A town where the circus is visiting.

Characters: Oliver the elephant, the circus owner, and the people of the town

Plot: Oliver the elephant was supposed to join the circus, but the circus owner only ordered ten elephants, and Oliver was number eleven getting off the boat. He tries numerous ways to find a home, but nothing seems to work out for him.

Solution: Oliver is really very talented, and eventually the circus owner gives him a job.

Summary: Oliver the elephant is left all alone at the shipping dock because the circus owner did not order eleven elephants, but only ten. Oliver doesn't know where to go. A mouse suggests he try the zoo, but they do not need an elephant either. He tries being a pet, but most people already have pets. He tries being a dog for a lady, but she has no hay for him to eat. He tries being a horse, but he cannot jump the fence. He passes a playground where he plays with the children, and they have a wonderful time! At rest time, they talk about what they want to be when they grow up. When it's Oliver's turn, he tells them he wants to be a dancing elephant, and he dances for the children. Many people stop to watch because he is so good. The circus parade happens to be coming down the street, and no one pays any attention to it—they're too busy watching Oliver dance. When the circus owner sees what is happening, he changes his mind and decides he does need Oliver in the circus after all.

Curriculum Connections: Pet unit, circus unit, character education—determination

ACTIVITIES FOR MEDIA SPECIALISTS

Schema

Ask the students if they have ever seen an elephant walking around all by itself. Explain that only if they travel to Africa or Asia would they be able to see an elephant walking around alone in the wild. They will not see one walking down a city street in America. Ask what they know about elephants. Correct any misconceptions.

Predicting

Show students the cover of the book. Ask what they think the story might be about. Show them the pictures of the circus acts. Ask how these two scenes might be connected.

Visualizing

Ask students to do the following exercise: Close your eyes and picture yourself sliding down an elephant's trunk. What does it feel like? Did you like it? Why or why not?

Library Skills

Tell students the following: The author of this book is Syd Hoff. He has written other stories that you can read all by yourself. Where would you find his books?

ACTIVITIES FOR TEACHERS

Decoding

The students may need to review or decode the following words from the story.

mistake	ordered	moving	followed
drivers	weighing	heavy	pretend

Phonics

Review the –unk word family.

dunk	bunk	trunk	sunk
skunk	chunk	stunk	shrunk

Phonemic Awareness

Review rhyming by having the children draw pictures of the some of the words with the –unk word family.

Fluency

Have the students repeat the following poem:

> There once was a skunk,
>
> Who hid in my bunk,
>
> So I hid in my trunk,
>
> But he still really stunk.

Comprehension

Recall

Which animal tries to help Oliver first? *A mouse.*

Why did the peanut man give Oliver some peanuts? *He was being honest.*

Why couldn't the people along the street keep Oliver for a pet? *They already had pets.*

Why couldn't Oliver be a horse for the man? *He couldn't jump fences.*

Why didn't anyone pay attention to the circus parade? *They were watching Oliver dance.*

Inferring

Why did the lady on the scale say she was as heavy as an elephant? *It's just an expression.*

Do you think Oliver wanted to be a different kind of animal? Why or why not? *Accept any reasonable answers.*

Was Oliver a good playmate? *Accept any reasonable answers.*

Synthesizing

Design a piece of playground equipment in the shape of an elephant and show the types of activities that can be done on it.

WRITING ACTIVITIES

Main Idea

Write the main idea of the story in one sentence.

_____

_____

_____

Sequencing

Number the following events in the order they happened in the story.

_____ Oliver pretends to be a pet dog for a lady.

_____ Oliver goes to the zoo, but the zoo man does not need an elephant.

_____ Oliver is needed in the circus after all.

_____ Oliver comes across the ocean with ten other elephants.

_____ Oliver tries to be a jumping horse.

Story Elements

Who are the main characters? _____

Where does the story take place? _____

What is the problem? _____

How is the problem solved? _____

Compare and Contrast

Compare Oliver to the horses. How are they alike? How are they different?

_____

_____

_____

_____

Summarizing

Write a summary of the story on another piece of paper.

PARENTS' PAGE

Dear Parents,

We have just finished reading *Oliver* by Syd Hoff. Oliver the elephant is left all alone at the shipping dock because the circus owner did not order eleven elephants, but only ten. Oliver doesn't know where to go. A mouse suggests he try the zoo, but they do not need an elephant either. He tries being a pet, but most people already have pets. He tries being a dog for a lady, but she has no hay. He tries being a horse, but he cannot jump the fence. He passes a playground where he plays with the children, and they have a wonderful time! At rest time, they talk about what they want to be when they grow up. When it's Oliver's turn, he tells them he wants to be a dancing elephant, and he dances for them. Many people stop to watch because he is so good. The circus parade happens to be coming down the street, and no one pays any attention to it—they're too busy watching Oliver dance. When the circus owner sees what is happening, he changes his mind and decides he does need Oliver in the circus after all.

The following activities provide additional ways to enhance your child's learning experience.

Enrichment Activities

A visit to the zoo is always fun for kids. Elephants could be the focal point for a trip after reading this story. It might be fun for your child to sketch a drawing while watching an elephant. Some zoos even have elephant rides!

Using modeling clay, work with your child to make your very own elephant. Give it a name.

The following books may be of interest to your child:

Elmer the Elephant by David McKee

Elmer and the Kangaroo by David McKee

Uncle Elephant by Arnold Lobel

Horton Hears a Who! by Dr. Seuss

Horton Hatches the Egg by Dr. Seuss

The Blind Man and the Elephant by Jean Richards

Have your child write about or draw a real or make-believe elephant.

Oscar Otter

by Nathaniel Benchley
Reading Level 2.6

Setting: The woods

Characters: Oscar the Otter, his father, the beaver, the fox, the wolf, and the moose

Plot: Oscar loves sliding down the hill into the water, but the beaver is always cutting down trees to build dams in the water. Then Oscar crashes into them. Oscar decides to build a secret slide all the way up the mountain but gets into trouble when a fox wants Oscar for supper!

Solution: Oscar slides down his secret slide to escape.

Summary: Oscar the Otter loves to slide into the pond, but the beaver has to build his home there, and the trees he chews down are in Oscar's way. So Oscar goes way up the mountain to build a secret slide, even though his father warns him not to got too far away from the water because other animals might catch him. But Oscar is determined. He climbs very high, builds his slide, and slides down at the end of each day. One day, he looks around and decides to explore. Little does he know, but a fox is watching him, as are a wolf, a mountain lion, and a moose. Soon the chase is on, and Oscar slides to safety with the help of the beaver, who has made a ramp over his logs so that Oscar can glide right into the pond. All the other animals crash into the log. The beaver saves the day!

Curriculum Connections: Animal unit, food chain, character education—respect for adults

ACTIVITIES FOR MEDIA SPECIALISTS

Schema

Ask students if they have ever seen an otter. Explain that there are river otters as well as ocean otters. They are very playful creatures and fun to watch.

Predicting

Show students the picture of the fox, wolf, and mountain lion crashing into the tree. Ask what they think happened.

Visualizing

Ask students to do the following exercise: Picture yourself at the top of a very high water slide. Now get ready, get set, slide! How does that feel?

Library Skills

Have a book with a call number for each letter of the alphabet for every child. Give each child a book. Call out the alphabet and have the students line up according to the call number on their book, as the books would be placed on the shelves.

ACTIVITIES FOR TEACHERS

Decoding

The students may need to review or decode the following words from the story:

corner	idea	build	happened
replied	through	interesting	explore
watched	believe	leaped	hurried

Phonics

Review the short and long sounds of /ea/.

leap	please	beaver	mean	heat	team
great	head	read	tread	thread	spread

Phonemic Awareness

Say the following words and have the students tell you the sound in the middle.

leaf	slide	smack	down	catch
need	took	him	like	fox
flash	zoom	ramp	crash	time

Comprehension

Recall

Why was Oscar Otter so mad at the beaver? *He blocked his slide with a tree.*

Why did Oscar's father warn him not to go too far from the water? *Because water was his protection from other animals.*

Why was Oscar going to keep his slide a secret? *So other animals wouldn't catch him.*

Why did the moose just walk away from the other animals during the chase? *He thought they were all crazy.*

Why didn't Oscar go back up the mountain? *He was happy at home not being chased.*

Inferring

Why do you think the beaver helped Oscar as he came flying down the hill? *Accept any reasonable answer.*

Why do you think Father let Oscar go up the mountain? *He believed Oscar needed to learn a lesson on his own.*

Do you think the fox, the wolf, and the mountain lion will try to chase Oscar again? Why or why not? *Accept any reasonable answer.*

Synthesizing

Create a word-search puzzle using words from the story.

WRITING ACTIVITIES

Main Idea

Write the main idea of the story in one sentence.

_____

_____

_____

Sequencing

Number the following events in the order they happened in the story.

_____ Oscar builds his own secret slide.

_____ Beaver helps Oscar slide into the pond.

_____ Beaver chews down trees to build his winter home.

_____ Oscar is chased by a fox, a wolf, a mountain lion, and a moose.

_____ Oscar Otter plays with the other otters on the otter slide.

Story Elements

Who are the main characters? _____

Where does the story take place? _____

What is the problem? _____

How is the problem solved? _____

Compare and Contrast

Compare the moose and the mountain lion. How are they alike? How are they different?

_____

_____

_____

_____

Summary

Write a summary of the story on another piece of paper.

PARENTS' PAGE

Dear Parents,

We just finished reading *Oscar the Otter* in class. Oscar loves to slide into the pond, but the beaver has to build his home there, and the trees he chews down are in Oscar's way. So Oscar goes way up the mountain to build a secret slide, even though his father warns him not to got too far away from the water because other animals might catch him. But Oscar is determined. He climbs very high, builds his slide, and slides down at the end of each day. One day, he looks around and decides to explore. Little does he know, but a fox is watching him, as are a wolf, a mountain lion, and a moose. Soon the chase is on, and Oscar slides to safety with the help of the beaver, who has made a ramp over his logs so that Oscar can glide right into the pond. All the other animals crash into the log. The beaver saves the day!

Enrichment Activities

There are several very interesting animals in this story. It may be possible to see them in a zoo or a wildlife habitat area. It is especially interesting to learn about the beaver and how it builds a home.

This is a great story to make the point that children must listen to their parents because it is parents' job to keep them safe. Ask your child what could have happened to the little otter. Continue the discussion with things you do to keep your child safe.

If it is wintertime, it would be fun to build a slide like the otter. If it is summertime or the weather is warm, a trip to a water park would provide your student with the same kind of experience the otter had sliding down his slide.

The following books might be of interest to your child.

Nonfiction

Kip the Sea Otter by Bonnie Taylor

Otter by Sandy Ransford

Sea Otter by Lynn M. Stone

Tilly: A River Otter by Bonnie Taylor

Fiction

Flatfoot Fox and the Case of the Nosy Otter by Clifford Eth

Owl at Home

by Arnold Lobel
Reading Level 2.2

Setting: The home of Owl

Character: Owl

Plot: Owl lives happily in his home, but he continually encounters strange situations, partly of his own making. First, it's winter inside his house, then strange bumps appear in his bed, there's a pot full of tears, he has to race against himself up and down his stairs, and then there's a friendly moon.

Solution: Owl learns some lessons the hard way, but sometimes he learns nothing at all.

Summary: Owl has some ideas about how to get along with nature and make his home even more comfortable and perfect. However, he does some silly things to try and make things go his way. The reader will chuckle at his foolishness. First, when he tries to be nice to Old Man Winter, he has a problem. Then when he tries to figure out what the strange bumps in his bed are, he makes himself uncomfortable. When he makes a special tea, he learns about salty tears. When he tries to be in two places at once, he realizes it is impossible. When he tries to say good night to the moon, he finds comfort in the fact that the moon does not go away.

Curriculum Connections: Animal unit, foolishness theme, solar system unit

ACTIVITIES FOR MEDIA SPECIALISTS

Schema

Ask students the following questions:

What kind of animal is an owl?

When do they sleep and eat?

Owls can turn their head 360 degrees. How?

Visualizing

Ask students to do the following exercises:

Picture yourself in the coziest place in your home. Tell about your cozy place.

Have you ever wished you could be in two places at the same time—for example, soccer practice and a birthday party? Is that possible? How have you solved a problem like this in the past?

Fluency

Read aloud the beginning of Chapter 4, "Upstairs and Downstairs," up to the sentence, "But he could not be in both places at once." Model reading of the phrases. Have your voice go up when Owl goes upstairs and down when Owl goes downstairs. Ask volunteers to copy the way you read the phrases, and then have everyone repeat it together as a group.

Library Skills

Ask students: How many chapters are in this book? Where do you look to find out without flipping through the whole book? Where is the table of contents in a book? Arnold Lobel, the author, has written many books for children. Where in the library media center would you find other books by this author?

ACTIVITIES FOR TEACHERS

Decoding

The students may need to review or decode the following words from the story:

pounding	knocking	thumping
against	whooshed	pleasant
cupboard	sobbed	perhaps
answer	farther	pajamas

Phonics

Start with the word *owl*. Add a beginning sound to make a new word. Change the ending and beginning to make new words using the phoneme "ow."

fowl	how	sow	down
howl	now	wow	town
jowl	cow	bow	brown
yowl	clown	drown	

Phonemic Awareness

Demonstrate to the students how two short words can go together to make a longer word.

down-town	up-stairs	down-stairs
out-side	fire-place	hall-way
cup-board	sea-shore	every-one

Recall

In the first chapter, why does Owl think someone is knocking and banging at his door? *The wind was making the door bang open and shut.*

What happens to Owl's bed in the second chapter? *Owl gets so upset about the two bumps that he jumps up and down on the bed and breaks it.*

In Chapter 3, why was Owl thinking about so many sad things and crying? *He needed tears to make tear-water tea.*

What did Owl learn in Chapter 4, "Upstairs and Downstairs"? *He learned that you cannot be in two places at once.*

Why did Owl think the moon was following him home? *Because it was getting higher in the sky.*

Inferring

Do you think it was a good idea for Owl to invite winter into his house? Why or why not? *No, it was too cold.*

Do you think this is the first time there have been bumps in Owl's bed? If not, why couldn't he sleep on this particular night? *Accept any reasonable answers.*

Do you think Owl had a good solution to his problem in the chapter titled "Upstairs and Downstairs"? *Accept any reasonable answers.*

Synthesizing

Design a home for Owl so that he won't have any of the problems that he had in this book. What kind of books could Owl read so that he would understand more about the world around him?

WRITING ACTIVITIES

Main Idea

Write the main idea of the story in one sentence.

_____

_____

_____

Sequencing

Number the following events in the order they happened in the story.

_____ Owl thinks unhappy thoughts to make himself cry.

_____ The moon follows Owl home.

_____ Owl has bumps at the bottom of his bed.

_____ Owl runs up and down the stairs.

_____ A guest bangs and pounds at Owl's door.

Story Elements

Who are the main characters? _____

Where does the story take place? _____

What is the problem? _____

How is the problem solved? _____

Compare and Contrast

Compare Owl's home with your home. How are they alike? How are they different?

_____

_____

_____

_____

Summary

Write a summary of the story on another piece of paper.

PARENTS' PAGE

Dear Parents,

We have just finished reading a story titled *Owl at Home* by Arnold Lobel. It is a beginning chapter book with five chapters. Owl is very happy is his cozy home in the woods. However, when he tries to be nice to Old Man Winter, he has a problem. Then when he tries to figure out what the strange bumps in his bed are, he makes himself uncomfortable. When he makes a special tea, he learns about salty tears. When he tries to be in two places at once, he realizes it is impossible. When he tries to say good night to the moon, he finds comfort in the fact that the moon does not go away.

The following activities provide additional ways to enhance your child's learning experience.

Enrichment Activities

Visit a nature center or zoo where your child can observe a real owl. There may be many species to see. Have your child choose a favorite one and sketch a picture of it.

Have your child write in a journal about the trip.

Together with your child, write another chapter to this book. Remember, sometimes Owl is not as wise as he should be.

Make a board game. Draw a picture of an owl in some of the squares on the board. If you land on the owl square, you have to go back to home.

Have your child write a letter to Owl and ask him to come visit your house.

Have your child write a story or draw a picture of himself or herself and Owl doing something together that they enjoy.

The following books may be of interest to your child.

Fiction

Owl Moon by Jane Yolen

Good-night, Owl! by Pat Hutchins

The Owl & the Pussycat by Edward Lear (poem)

Nonfiction

Owl Babies Martin Waddel

Baby Owl Aubrey Lang

Porcupine's Pajama Party

by Terry Webb Harshman
Reading Level 2.5

Setting: Porcupine's house

Characters: Porcupine, Owl, and Otter

Plot: Porcupine is eating lunch when he realizes he is lonely. He invites his friends to a pajama party, and they all reveal their secret fears.

Solution: After watching a scary movie, Porcupine, Owl and Otter all discover what they think are monsters in the dark. When they team up and discover that their imaginations are creating the monsters, they relax and have a restful night.

Summary: In the first chapter, "The Invitations," Porcupine decides to invite his friends, Owl and Otter, over for a pajama party. He writes out the invitations and delivers them, but neither friend is home. He waits and waits and becomes worried. Then finally, the phone rings. Owl wants to come, but he also wants to watch *Monster Bat* on television. Porcupine tells him to come watch it at his house. Otter wants to bake cookies so he takes the recipe to Porcupine's house. They make the cookies but eat too much dough. After watching the movie, they try to go to sleep, but they are all afraid of their own monsters. Eventually, they help each other discover what the real "monsters" are.

Curriculum Connections: Animal unit, friendship unit, being brave theme

ACTIVITIES FOR MEDIA SPECIALISTS

Schema

Ask students what they know about real porcupines, owls, and otters. How many have ever had a pajama party or sleepover? Ask: What do you do? Do you tell scary stories or watch scary movies? What has happened?

Predicting

Ask students to talk about the following: What might happen at a pajama party with an owl, a porcupine, and an otter? Look at the picture on the cover of the book. Why do you think owl is covering his eyes? What do the looks on the faces of the three friends tell you about the story?

Visualizing

As students to do the following exercise: Picture yourself in different house after you have watched a scary movie. How do you think you might feel?

Library Skills

Show the students pictures of real owls, otters, and porcupines and the fictional characters in the book. Have them explain why the picture could be either fiction or nonfiction. Ask them to list other ways one can tell whether a book is fiction or nonfiction.

ACTIVITIES FOR TEACHERS

Decoding

The students may need to review or decode the following words from the story:

sandwiches	giggled	shivered	recipe
promised	squeezed	measure	dough
tastier	delicious	stupendous	sheriff
croaked	slithery	imagine	snuggled

Phonics

Have the students add the endings to make new words by adding "–ed" and "–ing" to words.

laugh	laughed	laughing
howl	howled	howling
scream	screamed	screaming
flip	flipped	flipping
tap	tapped	tapping

Phonemic Awareness

Clap out the syllables of the words listed in the Phonics section.

Comprehension

Recall

What did Porcupine do while he waited for Owl and Otter to call back about the invitation? *He drank tea.*

Why would it be more fun to watch the movie together? *It is fun to get scared together.*

Why did the recipe for cookies only make three cookies? *The friends ate too much of the dough.*

Why did Owl become frightened when the others went to the bathroom? *He was alone.*

How did the friends solve each other's fears? *They uncovered the reasons behind the other's fear.*

Inferring

Why did Porcupine become worried when his friends did not respond to his invitation? *He was afraid they did not want to come to his party.*

Why do you think the friends were so scared when they went to bed that night? *Because they watched a scary movie and it put ideas in their heads.*

Synthesizing

Pretend you are going to have a pajama party. Design an invitation. Who will you invite? Make plans for the evening. Think up some fun things to do.

WRITING ACTIVITIES

Main Idea

Write the main idea of the story in one sentence.

_____

_____

_____

Sequencing

Number the following events in the order they happened in the story.

_____ The three friends watch a scary movie.

_____ A blanket scares Porcupine in the dark.

_____ Porcupine invites Otter and Owl to a pajama party.

_____ All the scary mysteries are solved, and the friends go to sleep.

_____ The three friends bake cookies together.

Story Elements

Who are the main characters? _____

Where does the story take place? _____

What is the problem? _____

How is the problem solved? _____

Compare and Contrast

Compare the three friends. How are they alike? How are they different?

_____

_____

_____

_____

Summarizing

Write a summary of the story on another piece of paper.

PARENTS' PAGE

Dear Parents,

We have just finished reading a book called *Porcupine's Pajama Party*. This is an I Can Read Book with four chapters. In the first chapter, "The Invitations," Porcupine decides to invite his friends, Owl and Otter, over for a pajama party. He writes out the invitations and delivers them, but neither friend is home. He waits and waits and becomes worried. Then finally, the phone rings. Owl wants to come, but he also wants to watch *Monster Bat* on television. Porcupine tells him to come watch it at his house. Otter wants to bake cookies, so he takes the recipe to Porcupine's house. They make the cookie dough, but eat too much of it. After watching the movie, they try to go to sleep, but they are all afraid of their own "monsters." Eventually, they help each other discover what the real monsters are.

The following activities provide additional ways to enhance your child's learning experience.

Enrichment Activities

If your children have problems with "scary things in the night," this is a good story to help them understand what causes mysterious noises and figures in the dark. You might try showing them different objects in the dark, then turning on the lights to let your children see how different the objects appear in the light.

In one part of the book, all the animals want to sleep in the middle of the bed because they just finished watching a scary movie. Owl and Otter each give a good reason why they should sleep in the middle, but Porcupine says emphatically that he has three good reasons. He says, " It is *my* house, *my* pajama party, and *my* bed." Ask your child if he or she thinks this is a good way for a host or hostess to act. Why or why not?

Have a pajama party. This does not necessarily mean the kids stay all night.

The following books may be of help in solving nighttime fears:

Brave Little Monster by Ken Baker

Amanda Pig and the Awful, Scary Monster by Jean Van Leeuwen

Jessica Takes Charge by Linda LaRose

Monsters in Your Bed—Monsters in Your Head by Rainey

Encourage your child to write a story or draw a picture about a monster.

Pretty Good Magic

by Cathy East Dubowski and Mark Dubowski
Reading Level 2.4

Setting: The very quiet town of Forty Winks

Characters: Presto the Magician, the Mayor of Forty Winks, and dozens of rabbits

Plot: Presto the Magician is a pretty good magician, but he wants to be a *great* magician, which leads to an overpopulation of rabbits.

Solution: Presto reads a magic book and tries the "Rabbits by the Dozen" trick, which works a little too well, but he awakens the sleepy little town.

Summary: Presto the Magician arrives in the sleepy little town of Forty Winks and puts on a magic show. The mayor thanks Presto for his "pretty good magic." But Presto wants to do some really *great* magic, so he studies a new trick called "Rabbits by the Dozen." The trick doesn't work immediately, but the next morning, there are rabbits everywhere in Forty Winks. The mayor is upset that the rabbits have brought chaos to his nice, quiet town. The people of Forty Winks, however, are not sleepy and quiet anymore. They laugh and have fun. So Presto decides to open a magic school, and then everyone can learn the tricks, have fun, and take home a rabbit to practice the rabbit and the hat trick.

Curriculum Connections: Reading theme, hobbies, character education—determination

ACTIVITIES FOR MEDIA SPECIALISTS

Schema

Ask if anyone has seen a magician. What did the magician do? Ask if anyone has heard the saying "forty winks." Explain the use of the phrase.

Predicting

Show the students the picture in which the rabbits cause a traffic jam in Forty Winks. Ask what they think has happened in the quiet little town.

Visualizing

Have students do the following exercise: Picture yourself surrounded by dozens and dozens of rabbits hopping all over your yard. Would you be laughing, or would you be a little scared? What would you do?

Library Skills

Show the students where to find books on magic tricks in the library. Some students will undoubtedly get very interested in the topic.

ACTIVITIES FOR TEACHERS

Decoding

The students may need to review or decode the following words from the story:

newspaper	curtain	scarves	favorite
dozens	cousins	awful	snoring
tickled	believe	appear	raised
twitched	elevator	nervous	taught

Phonics

Have the students substitute the middle vowel in these words.

trick	hat	tall	deck
track	hut	tell	dock
truck	hit	toll	duck

Phonemic Awareness

Have the students repeat this chant and listen for the rhyming words.
"Calling all rabbits
and all of their cousins,
Rabbit-ca-dabra!
Dozens and dozens."

Comprehension

Recall

What four tricks did Presto do at his first show in town? *He turned three scarves into four, made a deck of cards fly, sawed a woman in half, and pulled a rabbit out of a hat.*

Why did Presto feel sad after the show? *He only did pretty good magic, not great magic.*

What did he do when he got back to his hotel? *He studied his magic book.*

What happened to the hat after Presto went to bed? *It started to shake and shake.*

How did Presto get the rabbits out of the hotel? *He sent them down on the elevator in three trips.*

What was Presto's great idea? *To start a magic school and give everyone a rabbit for the hat trick.*

Inferring

Do you think it was good that Presto came to the town of Forty Winks?

How do you think the mayor felt about Presto at the end of the story?

Synthesizing

Perform your own magic trick. You can find books of tricks in the library.

WRITING ACTIVITIES

Main Idea

Write the main idea of the story in one sentence.

_____

_____

_____

Sequencing

Number the following events in the order they happened in the story.

_____ The school children are sad when the rabbits leave.

_____ Every rabbit has its own magician.

_____ Presto reads his book of magic to learn a great trick.

_____ Presto looks in his magic book to learn how to send all the rabbits back to where they came from.

_____ A cloud of smoke comes out of Presto's black hat.

Story Elements

Who is the main character? _____

Where does the story take place? _____

What is the problem? _____

How is the problem solved? _____

Compare and Contrast

Compare the bed salesman to the usher in the movie. How are they alike? How are they different?

_____

_____

_____

_____

Summarizing

Write a summary of the story on another piece of paper.

PARENTS' PAGE

Dear Parents,

We have just finished reading *Pretty Good Magic.* In this entertaining book, Presto the Magician arrives in the sleepy little town of Forty Winks and puts on a magic show. The mayor thanks Presto for his "pretty good magic." But Presto wants to do some really *great* magic, so he studies a new trick called "Rabbits by the Dozen." The trick doesn't work immediately, but the next morning, there are rabbits all over in Forty Winks. The mayor is upset that the rabbits have brought chaos to his nice, quiet town. The people of Forty Winks, however, are not sleepy and quiet anymore. They laugh and have fun. So Presto decides to open a magic school, and then everyone can learn the tricks, have fun, and take home a rabbit to practice the rabbit and the hat trick.

The following activities provide additional ways to enhance your child's learning experience.

Enrichment Activities

There are stores that specialize in magic tricks. It might be fun to visit one and see what is available.

This book may spark an interest in magic in your children. The following books may be of interest.

Nonfiction

Amazing Math Magic by Oliver Ho

Card Tricks by Cynthia F. Klingel

Clever Close-up Magic by Bob Longe

Easy Card Tricks by Peter Arnold

Experiments with Magic by Salvatore Tocci

Kid's Magic Secrets: Simple Magic Tricks and Why They Work by Loris G. Bree

Simple Magic Tricks: Easy-to-Learn Magic Tricks with Everyday Objects by Jon Allen

World's Greatest Card Tricks by Bob Longe

Young Magician: Card Tricks by Oliver Ho

Young Magician: Magic Tricks by Oliver Ho

Fiction

Sylvester and the Magic Pebble by William Steig

Franklin and the Magic Show by Sharon Jennings

Big Anthony and the Magic Ring by Tomie dePaola

R Is for Radish

by Molly Coxe
Reading Level 2.6

Setting:	In the home and at the school in Radish's neighborhood
Characters:	Radish the Rabbit, Mrs. Mink the teacher, Pinky the Pig, and Kat the Cat
Plot:	Radish hates spelling, recess, show-offs, and flashlight tag
Solution:	Radish discovers various ways to solve her problems: spelling becomes fun, recess is a challenge, and showing off actually is not a bad thing when someone is a ham. Even flashlight tag becomes easy when Radish uses her common sense.
Summary:	In Chapter One, Radish the Rabbit does not like spelling, but when her sister listens to rap music, Radish picks up the beat and finds a fun way to remember her spelling words. In Chapter Two, Radish does not like recess, but her teacher helps her find an activity that fits her skills perfectly. In Chapter Three, Radish is afraid that show-off Pinky the Pig will ruin her play, but as it turns out, Pinky actually enhances the performance. In Chapter Four, Radish and her friends are playing flashlight tag, and Radish finds her friends when she realizes they will be drawn to the smell of the raspberry pie.

Curriculum Connections: Character education—overcoming problems, being creative

ACTIVITIES FOR MEDIA SPECIALISTS

Schema

Students know about spelling tests. Ask whether they like them and how they study for them.

Play a rap CD for students so that they will understand the beat and how it might help when learning to spell words. Ask what they do at recess. Why do they choose a particular activity?

Ask: Has anyone ever written or been in a play? Is it easy? What does it mean to be a "ham"?

Ask: Has anyone ever played flashlight tag? Explain how to do it.

Predicting

Show the students the cover of the book and ask what kind of character they think Radish is. Show the table of contents and point out how all the chapters begin with the letter R.

Visualizing

Ask students to do the following exercise: Make a picture in your head of the playground. Do you see many kids just standing around? Which is more fun, playing or standing around with nothing to do?

Fluency

Explain the scene in which Radish's sister is listening to rap music. Read the rap that Radish has made up. Have the students repeat it after you until they get a good rhythm going.

Library Skills

Ask students: If you wanted to find a book of plays or try to write a play yourself, what are some keywords you might use to search on the computer? *Theater, drama, plays, scripts, and so on.*

ACTIVITIES FOR TEACHERS

Decoding

The students may need to review or decode the following words from the story.

listening	slimy	slippery	toward
raspberry	blueberry	sparkle	perform
appeared	flashlight	searched	pricked

Phonics

Use Radish's spelling words to present or review the word families:

yuck	luck	muck	tuck	suck	stuck	cluck	truck	
junk	sunk	bunk	dunk	hunk	chunk	trunk	skunk	shrunk
pail	tail	mail	sail	rail	wail	frail	snail	quail	trail

Phonemic Awareness

Play Go Fish with either the vocabulary words or the phonics words. Have the students sound out each phoneme and have the other group members pronounce the word as a whole. If a student pronounces the word correctly, he or she gets to keep the card.

Comprehension

Recall

Chapter One: Rap

When did Radish start to study her spelling words for the spelling bee? *After dinner.*

What did Radish win when she won the spelling bee? *A banana split.*

Chapter Two: Recess

Why couldn't Radish play tetherball very well? *Her ears were too long.*

What was it that Radish could do really well? *Jump rope.*

Chapter Three: Rainbow

Why was Radish afraid to let Pinky be in her play? *She was afraid Pinky would hog the show.*

Why is it funny that Radish called Pinky "a ham"? *Ham comes from pigs.*

Chapter Four: Raspberry Pie

What game were Radish's friends playing? *Flashlight tag.*

How did Radish finally catch her friends? *She waited until they came to the smell of the pie.*

Inferring

How did Mrs. Mink figure out a good recess game for Radish? *She saw her jump over the ball.*

Why do you think the sunglasses helped Radish so she didn't "go blank" when trying to spell the words? *Answers will vary. They were a reminder of what she had practiced the night before.*

Synthesizing

Make up your own rap to help you remember your spelling words.

What other ways can you come up with to help you remember things?

WRITING ACTIVITIES

Main Idea

Write the main idea of the story in one sentence.

_____

_____

_____

Sequencing

Number the following events in the order they happened in the story.

_____ Radish and her friends play flashlight tag.

_____ Radish writes a play and performs it with Pinky.

_____ Rabbit raps her spelling words to make learning more fun.

_____ Rabbit learns to jump rope at recess.

_____ Rabbit is bored just writing her spelling words over and over.

Story Elements

Who is the main character? _____

Where does the story take place? _____

What is the problem? _____

How is the problem solved? _____

Compare and Contrast

Compare Radish and Pinky. How are they alike? How are they different?

_____

_____

_____

_____

Summarizing

Write a summary of the story on another piece of paper.

PARENTS' PAGE

Dear Parents,

We have just finished reading the book *R Is for Radish* by Molly Coxe. This is a four-chapter book. Radish is a rabbit who has some problems. In Chapter One, Radish the Rabbit does not like spelling, but when her sister listens to rap music, Radish picks up the beat and finds a fun way to remember her spelling words. In Chapter Two, Radish does not like recess, but her teacher helps her find an activity that fits her skills perfectly. In Chapter Three, Radish is afraid that show-off Pinky the Pig will ruin her play, but as it turns out, Pinky actually enhances the performance. In Chapter Four, Radish and her friends are playing flashlight tag, and Radish finds her friends when she realizes they will be drawn to the smell of the raspberry pie.

The following activities provide additional ways to enhance your child's learning experience.

Enrichment Activities

Play the game Scrabble. This is a great game for building vocabulary and spelling.

Help your child make up some rap songs to remember spelling words.

Take turns scrambling the letters of words and then having the other person put them back in order to make a word.

On the cover of the book, Radish is painting a sign to mark the radishes in her garden. Have your child make signs for your garden.

An alphabet book is fun to make. Think up a word for every letter, and make illustrations to match the word.

Read some books about real rabbits such as the following:

Rabbits by Zuza Vrbova

Rabbit by Stephen Savage

Cottontail Rabbits by Kristin Gallagher

The Life Cycle of a Rabbit by Lisa Trumbauer

Me and My Pet Rabbit by Christine Morley

Have your child write a story or draw a picture of himself or herself with Radish, doing something they enjoy.

Sammy the Seal

by Syd Hoff
Reading Level 2.0

Setting: A zoo in the city and a school

Characters: Sammy the Seal, the zoo animals, and the kids at school

Plot: Sammy the Seal loves his home at the zoo, but he is sad because he really wants to see what is on the outside as well.

Solution: The zookeeper allows Sammy to go outside the zoo because he has been a good seal.

Summary: It is time for Mr. Johnson to feed the animals at the zoo. He tends to the lions, elephants, monkeys, bears, and seals. All the animals are very happy, except for one sad seal named Sammy. He is sad because he wants to leave the zoo and explore the city. Mr. Johnson lets Sammy go because he has been such a good seal. Sammy looks up at the skyscrapers, down at a manhole, and into a restaurant. He talks to people on the street. When he becomes hot and thirsty, he cannot find enough water to jump into, until he spots a bathtub in a house and jumps right in. Then he sees children going to school and decides that school would be fun to try. The teacher finally lets him stay, and Sammy learns to read, write, and play volleyball (which he does very well). All the children want him to come back the next day, but Sammy decides that there is "no place like home."

Curriculum Connections: Animal unit, zoo unit; discussion of sayings ("no place like home"); character education—everyone has a special talent

ACTIVITIES FOR MEDIA SPECIALISTS

Schema

Ask how many children have ever been to the zoo. What was their favorite animal? Has anyone ever seen a seal? In the zoo? In the ocean?

Predicting

Show the students the cover of the book. Ask what they see. Ask if this story takes place in the country or in the city. Why do they think a seal is walking down the street with the children? Be sure they understand that this is a fictional story.

Visualizing

Ask students to do the following exercise: Picture yourself in a cage. How do you feel? What would it be like?

Library Skills

Discuss the parts of a book: the cover, spine, spine label, and title page.

ACTIVITIES FOR TEACHERS

Decoding

The students may need to review or decode the following words from the story.

hooray	basket	empty	wrong	around
stranger	guess	puddle	waiting	voices

Phonics

Review the "–ate" word family.

date	mate	fate	gate	hate
rate	plate	slate	state	

Phonemic Awareness

The first few pages of this book begin with a repetitive sentence. Divide the kids up into lions, elephants, monkeys, bears, and seals and then repeat the following sentences: "The lions ate their meat. The elephants ate their hay. The monkeys ate their bananas. The bears ate their honey. The seals ate their fish."

Comprehension

Recall

What was Mr. Johnson's job? *His job was to feed the animals.*

Why was Sammy unhappy at the zoo, when all the other animals were happy? *He wanted to see what was outside the zoo.*

Why did Mr. Johnson let Sammy go outside the zoo? *Because Sammy had been so good.*

Sammy met a lady on the street. What kind of coat did she like? *A fur coat.*

Where were the goldfish? *They were in the pet shop.*

Inferring

Why did the man say Sammy must be from out of town? *Because he was gawking at the skyscrapers like he had never seen one before.*

Do you think Sammy was a good student in school? Why or why not? *Yes, he was a good student because he paid attention to the teacher and was a fast learner.*

Synthesizing

What other games would Sammy be good at? *Basketball, soccer, and so on.*

WRITING ACTIVITIES

Main Idea

Write the main idea of the story in one sentence.

_____

_____

_____

Sequencing

Number the following events in the order they happened in the story.

_____ Sammy hurries back to the zoo to tell everyone about his adventures.

_____ Sammy looks all around the city.

_____ Sammy goes to school and learns to read.

_____ It is feeding time at the zoo.

_____ Sammy the Seal is unhappy.

Story Elements

Who are the main characters? _____

Where does the story take place? _____

What is the problem? _____

How is the problem solved? _____

Compare and Contrast

Compare the teacher to the zookeeper. How are they alike? How are they different?

_____

_____

_____

_____

Summarizing

Write a summary of the story on another piece of paper.

PARENTS' PAGE

Dear Parents,

We have just finished reading the book *Sammy the Seal* by Syd Hoff. Here is a summary of the story. It is time for Mr. Johnson to feed the animals at the zoo. He tends to the lions, elephants, monkeys, bears, and seals. All the animals are very happy, except for one sad seal named Sammy. He is sad because he wants to leave the zoo and explore the city. Mr. Johnson lets Sammy go because he has been such a good seal. Sammy looks up at the skyscrapers, down at a manhole, and into a restaurant. He talks to people on the street. When he becomes hot and thirsty, he cannot find enough water to jump into, until he spots a bathtub in a house and jumps right in. Then he sees children going to school and decides that school would be fun to try. The teacher finally lets him stay, and Sammy learns to read, write, and play volleyball (which he does very well). All the children want him to come back the next day, but Sammy decides that there is "no place like home."

The following activities provide additional ways to enhance your child's learning experience.

Enrichment Activities

This story can be used to start a discussion with your child about the sayings "the grass is always greener on the other side of the fence" and "there's no place like home." Tell your child about some of your own experiences related to these sayings. Encourage your child to talk about a time when either one of the sayings might have applied to his or her experiences. What did your child learn?

A trip to the zoo is always a fun and educational experience. This would be a good time to focus on the seals and observe them while they are being fed. Take pictures of the seals, and let your child take them to school to share with other students.

Visit a pet shop to learn what kinds of food different animals eat. Many pet shops carry good books as well.

The following Web sites might be of interest:

> http://www.zoobooks.com
> http://www.animal.discovery.com

The following books may be of interest:

> *Seals and Sea Lions* by John Bonnet
> *Seals* by Emily Rose Townsend
> *Seals* by Wayne Lynch
> *Seals* by Ron Hirschi

Scruffy

by Peggy Parish

Reading Level 1.9

Setting: Todd's house and the animal shelter

Characters: Todd, his mother, his father, and Mrs. Star at the shelter

Plot: Choosing a new pet at the animal shelter is not as easy as one might think.

Solution: Todd really doesn't decide which cat to take home—the cat decides for him.

Summary: It is Todd's birthday, and all he really cares about is the present he will get when the family visits the animal shelter. When they get to the shelter, Mrs. Star shows them all the cats. Todd has a really hard time making a choice between the cute, little kittens and a scruffy-looking cat with a crooked tail that has been there for a month. Mrs. Star explains that they can't keep all the cats indefinitely. Scruffy actually chooses Todd because they need each other.

ACTIVITIES FOR MEDIA SPECIALISTS

Schema

Ask the group the following questions: How many of you have pets? How many found your pet at an animal shelter? Why do we need animal shelters? How many of you have cats?

Have a few children tell about their experience at an animal shelter.

Predicting

Show the first picture in the book of Todd running into the kitchen and his mom holding a stack of pancakes with a candle on them. Ask students to predict what this picture might have to do with the picture on the cover of the book.

Visualizing

Ask students to do the following exercise: Think about the day you first saw your pet. How did you feel? What did you do to get ready for your pet? Picture rows and rows of cages with cats in them. That is what an animal shelter would look like.

Library Skills

Ask students where they would look to find a nonfiction book about how to care for kittens and cats. Ask what term would give them the best chance to find the right book: "cats" or "cat care"?

ACTIVITIES FOR TEACHERS

Decoding

The students may need to review or decode some of the following words from the story:

scratching	finally	building
choose	doorbell	punished
handsome	tumbled	crooked

Phonics

Have the students make as many words as they can by changing the beginning and ending sounds of "cat."

Phonemic Awareness

Pronounce the following two-syllable words and have the students say the entire word after you to promote fluency.

Teacher	*Student*
pre-sent	present
can-dle	candle
pack-age	package
shel-ter	shelter
sur-prise	surprise

Comprehension

Recall

What were some of the presents that Todd unwrapped? *Supplies to take care of the cat.*

What kind of animals did Mrs. Star have at the animal shelter? *Dogs, cats, birds, rabbits, snakes, and a monkey.*

What kinds of cats were in the cages? *Big ones, little ones, fat ones, skinny ones.*

Inferring

Why do you think the trip to the animal shelter seemed to "take forever"? *It always seems that way when one is anticipating something wonderful.*

What do you think it meant when Mrs. Star told Todd that people "get tired of their pets"?

Why do you think the older black and white kitten turned his back on Todd?

Why do you think the older black and white kitten didn't get held very much?

Synthesizing

What might be another way to take care of animals that people decide they don't want anymore?

WRITING ACTIVITIES

Main Idea

Write the main idea of the story in one sentence.

_____

_____

_____

Sequencing

Number the following events in the order they happened in the story.

_____ Todd looks at all the kittens but can't decide on one.

_____ Todd names his cat "Scruffy" and takes him home.

_____ Todd opens all his presents on his birthday.

_____ The old cat with the crooked tail gets mad at Todd.

_____ Todd and his parents go to the animal shelter to get a kitten.

Story Elements

Who are the main characters? _____

Where does the story take place? _____

What is the problem? _____

How is the problem solved? _____

Compare and Contrast

Compare the kittens with the old cat. How are they alike? How are they different?

_____

_____

_____

_____

Summarizing

Write a summary of the story on another piece of paper.

PARENTS' PAGE

Dear Parents,

We have just finished reading a book called *Scruffy*. It is a story about a boy named Todd who is having a birthday. All he really wants for his birthday is a cat. This book describes a trip to the animal shelter to pick out a cat for Todd. There is an interesting twist to the story in the end. We have worked on the harder words and practiced reading the story. Please have your child reread the story for you. Note any words that he or she does not read fluently and practice these by writing the words, using flash cards, or making a sentence with them. The following activities will enhance the story and the learning experience.

Enrichment Activities

Visit an animal shelter. Talk to the people who work there and have them explain how important their work is to the community.

If you have a pet, involve your children in the animal's care, even if it is only making sure the pet always has fresh water.

Some animals make good pets, and others do not. Discuss with your child which animals make good pets and why we leave other animals in the wild.

Visit a rescue center that helps injured wild animals get well and return to their natural habitat.

Check out nonfiction books on the care of animals such as:

How to Talk to Your Cat by Jean Craighead George

How to Talk to Your Dog by Jean Craighead George

Junior Pet Care Series by Zuzu Vrbova

Checkerboard Series by Stuart A. Kallen

Encourage your child to write a story or draw a picture of a pet you have or one he or she would like to have.

Sleepy Dog

by Harriet Ziefert
Reading Level 1.0

Setting: The home of a family of dogs, where a cat lives as well

Characters: Mother dog, a puppy, and a cat

Plot: This dog family has an unusual pet—a cat!

Solution: This cat and the puppy live in harmony because they are nice to each other.

Summary: In Chapter One, it is time to go to bed. Little Dog and Cat sleepily walk up the stairs to bed. Dog snuggles into bed, and Cat sleeps on top of the covers. Mother Dog comes in for a good-night kiss and turns out the light, then Cat and Dog go to sleep. In Chapter Two, Dog is dreaming that he is eating, and he is very happy. He also dreams that he is jumping over the moon and running. All the while, he smiles. Then he dreams he is being chased, and he smiles no more. He is scared—the dream wakes him up, and he needs a drink of water. Cat does too, and then they go back to bed. In Chapter Three, "The Clock," it's time to get up. Cat and Dog are happy to be able to play, and Little Dog is very happy to see his mother.

Curriculum Connections: Pet unit, friendship theme, concept of day and night, health unit—sleep is important to feel good

ACTIVITIES FOR MEDIA SPECIALISTS

Schema

Discuss with the children the idea that cats and dogs do not get along. Ask if they believe this is always the case. Ask students if anyone has both cats and dogs in the same house. Do they get along? Let students discuss their own experiences.

Predicting

Ask students what they think is going to happen in this story about a cat and dog.

Visualizing

Ask students to do the following exercise: Picture yourself sleeping. How do you look? Are you dreaming? What do you do if you wake up in the middle of the night?

Library Skills

Ask students the following questions: Is this a true (nonfiction) book about animals? How do you know? Where would you look for true books about animals? What do we call those books?

ACTIVITIES FOR TEACHERS

Decoding

The students may need to review some of the following words from the story:

pillow	night	light
sleep	sleepy	sleepyhead
dream	dreams	dreaming
jump	jumps	jumping
run	runs	running

Phonics

Use the clock chapter to review the –ick word family.

Tick	sick	nick	pick
flick	chick	click	

Phonemic Awareness

Read a selection of sentences from the book and ask the students how many words are in each sentence.

Comprehension

Recall

Where did Dog put his head when he went to bed? *On the pillow.*

Where was Cat when he and Dog went to bed? *On top of the covers.*

At night, what was turned on? *The moon.* What was turned off? *The light.*

Dog dreamed about four things. Can you name them? *Eating, jumping, running, and being chased.*

What did both Dog and Cat need when they woke up in the middle of the night? *A drink.*

In the morning, what turned off? *The moon and the clock.*

What turned on in the morning? *The sun and the light.*

Inferring

Why did dog wake up? *His dream scared him.*

Why were Dog and Cat so happy in the morning? *It was time to play.*

Synthesizing

Draw a picture of a dream you have had, or you can write a story about it.

WRITING ACTIVITIES

Main Idea

Write the main idea of the story in one sentence.

_____

_____

_____

Sequencing

Number the following events in the order they happened in the story.

_____ Sleepy Dog has a dream.

_____ The clock goes ring, ring, ring.

_____ Mother kisses Sleepy Dog good night.

_____ Sleepy Dog and Cat need a drink of water.

_____ Sleepy Dog puts his nose under the covers.

Story Elements

Who are the main characters? _____

Where does the story take place? _____

What is the problem? _____

How is the problem solved? _____

Compare and Contrast

Compare Sleepy Dog and Cat. How are they alike? How are they different?

_____

_____

_____

_____

Summarizing

Write a summary of the story on another piece of paper.

PARENTS' PAGE

Dear Parents,

We have just finished reading a book titled *Sleepy Dog* by Harriet Ziefert. There are four chapters in this beginning chapter book. In Chapter One, it's time to go to bed. Little Dog and Cat sleepily walk up the stairs to bed. Dog snuggles into bed, and Cat sleeps on top of the covers. Mother Dog comes in for a good-night kiss and turns out the light, then Cat and Dog go to sleep. In Chapter Two, Dog is dreaming that he is eating, and he is very happy. He also dreams that he is jumping over the moon and running. All the while, he smiles. Then he dreams he is being chased, and he smiles no more. He is scared—the dream wakes him up, and he needs a drink of water. Cat does too, and then they go back to bed. In Chapter Three, "The Clock," it's time to get up. Cat and Dog are happy to be able to play, and Little Dog is very happy to see his mother.

The following activities provide additional ways to enhance your child's learning experience.

Enrichment Activities

If you have a pet, discuss with your child why pets need love and affection just like humans. This is also an opportunity to take a trip to the animal shelter and perhaps even volunteer to help with the animals.

Discuss how animals can be helpful to elderly people who live alone. Maybe there is a neighbor or a relative who would appreciate a visit from you and a friendly dog. (Be sure there are no problems with allergies and that the animal is comfortable around new people.)

This is a good book to initiate a talk about time and clocks. With digital clocks so abundant, many children do not know how to tell time on a regular clock face. Check to make sure your child the concepts of AM and PM.

Additional Books

How to Talk to Your Cat by Jean Craighead George

How to Talk to Your Dog by Jean Craighead George

Dogs by Gail Gibbons

Read All about Dogs Series by Barbara J. Patten:

> *Canine Companions*
> *Dogs with a Job*
> *Hounds on the Trail*
> *Sporting Dogs*
> *The Terrier Breeds*
> *The World's Smallest Dog*

Small Pig

by Arnold Lobel
Reading Level: 1.8

Setting: A farm, the road to the city, and the city

Characters: A small pig, the farmer, and the farmer's wife

Plot: After the farmer's wife cleans up all the good, soft mud in his pigpen, Small Pig runs away to find another place with perfect mud, but he ends up in a sticky situation.

Solution: After Small Pig is rescued from the city and returns to the farm, it rains, and a new good, soft mud puddle is created.

Summary: Small Pig loves his good, soft mud puddle on the farm, but one day the farmer's wife decides to clean up the place—including the pigpen. Small pig misses his mud puddle so much that he runs away to look for another one. His search eventually takes him to the city, where he gets stuck in some new cement thinking it is mud. The farmer and his wife have been looking for him and come to his rescue.

Curriculum Connections: Pet unit, farm animal unit, character education unit—making good decisions

ACTIVITIES FOR MEDIA SPECIALISTS

Schema

Ask students:

Have you ever seen a junkyard? Describe it.

Does anyone have a pig stuffed animal? Let's discuss what you know about pigs.

Review the story of *The Three Little Pigs* that they know so well. Ask what other pig stories the students remember.

Prediction

Show the students the cover of the book and have them try to predict what the mud puddle has to do with the story.

Visualization

Ask students to do the following exercise: Close your eyes and picture yourself in a mud puddle. What would it feel like? How would it smell? Do you think you would like it? Why or why not?

Library Skills

Display both fiction and nonfiction titles about pigs and discuss the difference.

Demonstrate how one would find more books about pigs on the computer catalog.

Ask students: Who is Arnold Lobel? How would we find other books by Arnold Lobel?

ACTIVITIES FOR TEACHERS

Decoding

The students may need to review or decode some of the following words from the story:

barnyard	stable	coop	dirtiest
swamp	yourself	nearby	strange
crowd	happening	carefully	promise

Phonics

Have students build words with short /a/ as in *small* and short /i/ as in *pig* such as:

tall	call	pig	jig
fall	ball	dig	fig
mall	wall	twig	big

Fluency

Using page 32 of the book, have the students read what Small Pig says about cars and sofas. Encourage them to read with expression and change their tone of voice to match the picture.

Study the picture of the farmer and his wife on page 49. Next have students read the accompanying text, using their voices to express how they think the farmer and his wife would feel when the finally found their lost pig.

Comprehension

Recall

What kinds of items did Small Pig find in the junkyard? *See the pictures on pages 28–33.*

What did Small Pig see in the junkyard that made him want to leave? *A vacuum.*

Why didn't Small Pig know to stay out of good, soft mud in the city? *He couldn't read the "Keep Off" sign.*

Inferring

Why do you think Small Pig was so upset when his pigpen was clean? *The good, soft mud was gone.*

If the air was dirty in the city, did that mean there would be mud? What do you think Small Pig was thinking when he said that?

Why do you think so many people stopped to see Small Pig on the sidewalk? *They had never seen a pig stuck in the sidewalk before.*

Synthesizing

Do you think the farmer's wife will try to clean the pigpen again? Why or why not? *Accept any reasonable answer.*

Why did Small Pig move out of the swamp? Who helped him to make up his mind about moving on? *The dragonfly, the frog, the turtle, and the snake.*

WRITING ACTIVITIES

Main Idea

Write the main idea of the story in one sentence.

_____

_____

_____

Sequencing

Number the following events in the order they happened in the story.

_____ Small Pig leaves the swamp.

_____ The farmer and his wife find Small Pig.

_____ Small Pig lives in a pigpen on a farm.

_____ Small Pig leaves the farm because it is too clean.

_____ Small Pig leaves the junkyard and runs to the city.

Story Elements

Who are the main characters? _____

Where does the story take place? _____

What is the problem? _____

How is the problem solved? _____

Compare and Contrast

Compare the three friends. How are they alike? How are they different?

_____

_____

_____

_____

Summarizing

Write a summary of the story on another piece of paper.

PARENTS' PAGE

Dear Parents,

We have just finished reading *Small Pig* by Arnold Lobel. We have talked about what your child knows about pigs and junkyards. Small Pig loves his good, soft mud puddle on the farm, but one day the farmer's wife decides to clean up the place—including the pigpen. Small pig misses his mud puddle so much that he runs away to look for another one. His search eventually takes him to the city, where he gets stuck in some new cement, thinking it's mud. The farmer and his wife have been looking for him and come to his rescue.

The following activities provide additional ways to enhance your child's learning experience.

Enrichment Activities

If possible, let your child make a small mud puddle. Discuss how the mud feels and why a pig likes it so much.

Pigs have a bad reputation, but there are many wonderful stories with pigs as the main character at your library. For example:

Olivia by Ian Falconer

Olivia Saves the Circus by Ian Falconer

Olivia and the Missing Toy by Ian Falconer

Chester the Worldly Pig by Bill Peet

Poppleton by Cynthia Rylant

Starring Rosa by Otto Coontz

Read a nonfiction book about pigs such as *Pigs* by Gail Gibbons.

Encourage your child to draw a picture of or write about a pig that he or she would like to have for a pet.

The Smallest Cow in the World

by Katherine Paterson
Reading Level 2.8

Setting: Mr. Brock's dairy farm

Characters: Marvin; his mother, father, and sister, May; and Rosie, the meanest cow in the world

Plot: Marvin loves Rosie the cow, even though everyone else thinks she is the meanest cow in the world, but Marvin doesn't care. Marvin is extremely upset when the family must move. He is very unhappy, and no one can make him happy until he discovers "Rosie" again.

Solution: Marvin claims he has found Rosie but that a witch turned her into the smallest cow in the world. Rosie eventually helps him conquer his sadness and loneliness.

Summary: Rosie is the meanest cow on Brock's Dairy Farm, but Marvin, the son of the farm worker, loves Rosie. He thinks she is the most beautiful cow in the world. Mr. Brock decides he is too old to farm, and he sells Rosie and the farm. Marvin's Dad must find a new job. Marvin is extremely unhappy because Rosie is gone; he does not adjust to the move to a new farm. He acts out and then makes up a story about a witch who changed Rosie into the smallest cow in the world, saying he found her in the grass. The family goes along with his pretend Rosie because it makes him happy. But then school starts, and the kids make fun of him and Rosie. Finally, May comes up with a great idea—but it means Marvin has to leave Rosie at home. Marvin finally understands that he has a family who loves him and that he will never by lonely again.

Curriculum Connections: Farm unit, character education—respecting differences

ACTIVITIES FOR MEDIA SPECIALISTS

Schema

Depending on the location of your school, there may be many students who have a great deal of experience with farm animals. Knowing your school community will help you decide how much background information the children will have.

Predicting

Show the children the picture of Mr. Brock putting up the "For Sale" sign. Ask them what they think will happen. Explain that Mr. Brock is the owner of the farm and that Marvin's father works for Mr. Brock.

Visualizing

Ask students to do the following exercise: Picture yourself in a brand new school. What do you feel like? What would you do to make new friends?

Library Skills

Ask students: If you wanted to learn more about cows and farm animals, what section of the library do you think those books would be in? Review fiction and nonfiction. Review how to use the computer to find information.

ACTIVITIES FOR TEACHERS

Decoding

The students may need to review or decode some of the following words from the story:

switched	manure	except
scribbling	worried	thought
everywhere	imagination	peeped

Phonics

Have the children use the following words in a sentence:

smallest	meanest	saddest
loudest	biggest	loneliest
friendliest	happiest	smartest

Phonemic Awareness

Have the students orally change ending sounds to make new words.

hug *hut hum hub*
job *jot jog*
mad *mat map math*
sit *sip sis sill*

Fluency

At the beginning of the story, May tells Marvin all the reasons why she thinks Rosie is the meanest cow in the world. There is repetition, so the children can practice reading with fluency. It begins with May telling Marvin, "You don't feed her." Students could read this aloud in unison.

Comprehension

Recall

Marvin thinks Rosie became mean because of something Mr. Brock did to her. What was it? *He took away her calf.*

Marvin's family was sad because they had to move. How did everyone but Marvin become happier? *Dad found a new job, Mom started another garden, and May found a friend.*

How did Rosie become the smallest cow in the world? *The witch did it.*

Inferring

Who scribbled on the trailer, pulled up the flowers, and pulled all of May's books off the shelf? *Marvin, but he claimed it was Rosie.*

Why did Marvin do these bad things? *He was really miserable and lonely, and he wanted attention.*

Synthesizing

If you had an imaginary pet, what would it be? Make a house for your imaginary pet.

WRITING ACTIVITIES

Main Idea

Write the main idea of the story in one sentence.

_____

_____

_____

Sequencing

Number the following events in the order they happen in the story.

_____ Marvin plays with tiny Rosie all summer.

_____ May has to take care of Rosie, the meanest cow in the world.

_____ Marvin never has to be lonely again because tiny Rosie will always be with him.

_____ Marvin does bad things when the family moves.

_____ Mr. Brock sells the farm.

Story Elements

Who are the main characters? _____

Where does the story take place? _____

What is the problem? _____

How was is problem solved? _____

Compare and Contrast

Compare the big Rosie and the tiny Rosie. How are they alike? How are they different?

_____

_____

_____

_____

Summarizing

Write a summary of the story on another piece of paper.

PARENTS' PAGE

Dear Parents,

We have just finished reading the book *The Smallest Cow in the World* by Katherine Paterson. Rosie is the meanest cow on Brock's Dairy Farm, but Marvin, the son of the farm worker, loves Rosie. He thinks she is the most beautiful cow in the world. Mr. Brock decides he is too old to farm, and he sells Rosie and the farm. Marvin's Dad must find a new job. Marvin is extremely unhappy because Rosie is gone; he does not adjust to the move to a new farm. He acts out and then makes up a story about a witch who changed Rosie into the smallest cow in the world, saying he found her in the grass. The family goes along with his pretend Rosie because it makes him happy. But then school starts, and the kids make fun of him and Rosie. Finally, May comes up with a great idea, but it means Marvin has to leave Rosie at home. Marvin finally understands that he has a family who loves him and that he will never by lonely again. The following activities will extend and enhance your students study of the story.

Enrichment Activities

If your child is familiar with life on a farm, he or she understands how much work must be done. If not, it would be interesting to visit a working farm so your child can gain an appreciation of the kind of work that farmers do and the hard work involved to bring goods to the grocery store.

The following books might be of interest:

All the Places to Love by Patricia McLachlan

Barnyard Banter by Denise Fleming

And the Cow Said Moo by Mildred Phillips

Click, Clack Cows that Type by Doreen Cronin

Encourage your child to write a story about or draw a picture of a farm.

Stanley

by Syd Hoff
Reading Level 1.9

Setting: Prehistoric times in the land of the cavemen

Characters: Stanley the caveman, other cavemen, dinosaurs

Plot: Stanley is uncomfortable in his cave. He wants to find a more comfortable place to live. The other cavemen do not understand why he can't live like the rest of them do, but Stanley proves that being different has its advantages.

Solution: Stanley sets out to find a better place to live.

Summary: Stanley is a caveman who enjoys painting and planting seeds. He is uncomfortable sleeping on rocks, being cold, and fighting off bats. The other cavemen do not understand why he is unhappy with his living conditions, so they chase him away. Stanley tries to find the kind of place that's just right for him. Because he is kind and polite to the animals, they become his friends. He loves sleeping in the grass, but it is windy and sometimes it rains. Finally, he discovers how to stay out of the wind and rain: he builds a house! When he saves his old friends from the dinosaurs, they want him to come back to the cave. After Stanley shows them his house, they all build their own. Stanley shows them how to paint and plant and how to be nice to each other.

Curriculum Connections: Prehistoric times, character education—being different makes us unique

ACTIVITIES FOR MEDIA SPECIALISTS

Schema

Ask the children what they know about dinosaurs. Were there people on Earth during the time of the dinosaurs? How do they think cavemen slept? How do they think cavemen treated each other?

Predicting

Show the students the cover of the book. Ask if they think this is a true story. Point out the three cavemen up on the cliff. Have students discuss what they think is going on in this scene.

Visualizing

Ask students to do the following exercise: Picture yourself sleeping in a cave. What would it feel like?

Library Skills

Discuss the difference between a fiction and a nonfiction book. Display some dinosaur books. They are always a big hit.

ACTIVITIES FOR TEACHERS

Decoding

The students may need to review some of the following words from the story:

though	enough	tough
ground	answer	while
worse	snore	chimney
lonesome	carried	old-fashioned

Phonics

Use the word *cold* and have the students write new words by changing the beginning sound.

cold	bold	told
fold	sold	gold
hold	mold	

Phonemic Awareness

Pronounce the group of words in each line and have the children pick out the word that does not rhyme with the others:

cold	told	ten
fun	fold	bold
sold	sun	hold
old	mold	man
gold	cold	go

Fluency

Use the section of the book in which Stanley is looking for a place to live. Have one child each read the characters of Stanley, the bird, the fish, the worm, and the ape as reader's theater. Stop at the point when Stanley finds a field.

Comprehension

Recall

What three things did Stanley dislike about living in a cave? *A cave is cold, has hard rocks, and there are bats.*

Why did the other cavemen chase Stanley away? *Because he was different.*

Where did Stanley look for a new place to live? *He looked in a nest, in the water, on the ground, in a tree, and in space.*

Why didn't living in the field work for Stanley? *It was too windy and wet.*

Inferring

Why did Stanley get along with the animals so well but the other cavemen did not? *Stanley was very nice to the animals, and the other cavemen beat them with clubs.*

Why do you think Stanley tried many things that the other cavemen didn't? *Accept any reasonable answer. For example, he was a thinker, a risk taker, etc.*

Synthesizing

Now that Stanley has a place to live, he will need some furniture. How do you think he might furnish his new house? What else would he put in it besides furniture?

WRITING ACTIVITIES

Main Idea

Write the main idea of the story in one sentence.

_____

_____

_____

Sequencing

Number the following events in the order they happened in the story.

_____ The cavemen chase away Stanley.

_____ The other cavemen like the house Stanley built and build their own.

_____ Stanley builds a house in the field.

_____ The other cavemen want Stanley to act more like a caveman.

_____ Stanley searches everywhere for a place to live.

Story Elements

Who are the main characters? _____

Where does the story take place? _____

What is the problem? _____

How is the problem solved? _____

Compare and Contrast

Compare Stanley to the other cavemen. How are they alike? How are they different?

_____

_____

_____

_____

Summary

Write a summary of the story on another piece of paper.

PARENTS' PAGE

Dear Parents,

We have just finished reading the book *Stanley* by Syd Hoff. Stanley is a caveman who enjoys painting and planting seeds. He is uncomfortable sleeping on rocks, being cold, and fighting off bats. The other cavemen do not understand why he is unhappy with his living conditions, so they chase him away. Stanley tries to find the kind of place that's just right for him. Because he is kind and polite to the animals, they become his friends. He loves sleeping in the grass, but it is windy and sometimes it rains. Finally, he discovers how to stay out of the wind and rain: he builds a house! When he saves his old friends from the dinosaurs, they want him to come back to the cave. After Stanley shows them his house, they all build their own. Stanley shows them how to paint and plant and how to be nice to each other.

The following enrichment activities will further enhance the study of this book.

Enrichment Activities

If your child is interested in dinosaurs, this might be a good time to visit a natural history museum where exhibits explain how long ago dinosaurs roamed the Earth, as well when humans first appeared.

If your child liked this story, he or she will also like Danny and the Dinosaur books, which are also part of the An I Can Read Book series.

Stanley also lends itself well to a discussion about how to treat other people, as well as animals. If one is nice to others, usually others are nice in return.

Encourage your child to draw a picture that he or she would like to hang on the wall of your house.

The following books are selections about dinosaurs and prehistoric people that you may find at you school or public library.

Nonfiction

The Day of the Dinosaur by Stan and Jan Berenstain

Digging up Dinosaurs by Aliki

Dinosaur Time by Peggy Parish

Dinosaur Days by Joyce Milton and Richard Roe

Fiction

Little Grunt and the Big Egg by Tomie de Paola

Big Old Bones: A Dinosaur Tale by Donald and Carol Carrick

The Dinosaur Who Lived in My Backyard by B. G. Hennessy and Susan Davis

Three by the Sea

by Edward Marshall
Reading Level 1.8

Setting: The beach

Characters: Lolly, Spider, and Sam

Plot: After their picnic, the kids can't go for a swim right away, so they decide to tell stories. They are critical of each other's stories until Spider tells his.

Solution: Spider is last to tell his story and improves on the other two tales. He manages to satisfy everyone and have a good laugh, too.

Summary: Three friends are spending the day at the seashore. They have a picnic and feel too full to go swimming, so they decide to listen to Lolly's story from her reader about a rat and a cat. Spider and Sam decide that the story is dull, so Sam says he can do better. After he tells his story, Spider says he doesn't like the ending. So now it's Spider's turn, and he is going to make his story scary. His story takes a very interesting turn, and it does scare Lolly and Sam—even though they won't admit it. Spider really gets a good laugh out of the ending to his story.

Curriculum Connections: Ocean unit, storytelling unit, story writing

---

ACTIVITIES FOR MEDIA SPECIALISTS

Schema

Ask students if they have ever been to the ocean. Let them tell about their experiences to find out what they know about the sea.

Predicting

Tell the children that this is a "story within a story." Have them explain what they think that means.

Visualizing

Ask students to do the following exercise: Picture yourself with friends or family at the beach. What are you doing?

Library Skills

Show the students a variety of books from the shelves. Read the titles and have them decide if the book is fiction or nonfiction.

Make large cards with either fiction or nonfiction call numbers on them. Have the students line up as if they were books on a shelf.

ACTIVITIES FOR TEACHERS

Decoding

The students may need to review the following words from the story:

lemonade	true	brought	finish
shining	owner	catch	favorite
closer	cheese	sharp	asleep
tasty	juicy	tiptoed	scared

Phonics

Review contractions, their spelling and what words they stand for.

do not	don't	did not	didn't
cannot	can't	will not	won't
let us	let's	that is	that's
what is	what's	we will	we'll
it is	it's	I will	I'll
he is	he's	she is	she's

Phonemic Awareness

Clap out the syllables of the following words:

lemonade	picnic	story	better
finish	pretty	friend	owner
hungry	favorite	alone	closer
cheese	hooray	looked	monster

Comprehension

Recall

What did the three children have for their picnic? *They had hot dogs and lemonade.*

What did Lolly bring with her to the beach? *She brought her reader.*

What was it that made rat and cat friends? *They both liked cheese.*

Inferring

Why do you think Lolly insisted that Spider's story have a rat and a cat in it? *Because they were in her story, and Spider was trying to outdo her.*

Why do you think the pet shop owner questioned rat about wanting to buy a cat? *Chances are, the cat would eat the rat!*

Why did Lolly and Sam jump and yell "help!" *They were totally involved in Spider's story.*

Synthesizing

Create a story within a story like the one in this book.

WRITING ACTIVITIES

Main Idea

Write the main idea of the story in one sentence.

_____

_____

_____

Sequencing

Number the following events in the order they happened in the story.

_____ Sam tells a story about a rat that wanted a cat.

_____ The three by the sea go swimming.

_____ Lolly reads a story from her reader.

_____ Lolly, Spider, and Sam have a picnic on the beach.

_____ Spider tells a story about a sea monster.

Story Elements

Who are the main characters? _____

Where does the story take place? _____

What is the problem? _____

How is the problem solved? _____

Compare and Contrast

Compare Lolly, Sam, and Spider. How are they alike? How are they different?

_____

_____

_____

_____

Summary

Write a summary of the story on another piece of paper.

PARENTS' PAGE

Dear Parents,

We have just finished reading *Three by the Sea* by Edward Marshall. Three friends are spending the day at the seashore. They have a picnic and feel too full to go swimming right away, so they decide to listen to Lolly's story from her reader about a rat and a cat. Spider and Sam decide that the story is dull, so Sam says he can do better. After he tells his story, Spider says he doesn't like the ending. So now it's Spider's turn, and he is going to make his story scary. His story takes a very interesting turn, and it does scare Lolly and Sam—even though they won't admit it. The following activities will enhance your child's learning

Enrichment Activities

The beach may be a new experience for your child. If possible, consider visiting the ocean or a lake where your child can play on the beach.

If you have a sandbox, it is always fun for kids to build castles or other structures out of sand. They can be so creative!

This is a great book to encourage kids to tell stories. Have them practice a few times, perhaps in front of a mirror, and then record their story. Public speaking is frightening for many people, and this is a good way to build your child's confidence.

Emphasize that a story needs a strong beginning, middle, and end. Because your child's own experiences are familiar, they provide the good way for him or her to begin learning how to tell a tale.

The following books may be of interest to your child.

Nonfiction

> *Exploring the Deep, Dark Sea* by Gail Gibbons
>
> *Waves and Tides* by Patricia Armentrout
>
> *Follow the Water from Brook to Ocean* by Arthur Dorros
>
> *The Magic School Bus on the Ocean Floor* by Joanna Cole

Fiction

> *The Rainbow Fish* by Marcus Pfister
>
> *Rainbow Fish to the Rescue!* by Marcus Pfister
>
> *Rainbow Fish and the Big Blue Whale* by Marcus Pfister

Encourage your child to write a story about the ocean or draw a beautiful seascape.

Appendix

Reading Level	Title of Book	Author	Page
0.9	*Biscuit Goes to School*	Alyssa Satin Capucilli	13
1.0	*Sleepy Dog*	Harriet Ziefert	121
1.2	*And I Mean It, Stanley*	Crosby Bonsall	1
1.5	*Five Silly Fishermen*	Roberta Edwards	41
1.6	*Cave Boy*	Cathy East Dubowski and Mark Dubowski	25
1.6	*Ice-Cold Birthday*	Maryann Cocca-Leffler	57
1.7	*No More Monsters for Me!*	Peggy Parish	85
1.7	*Small Pig*	Arnold Lobel	125
1.8	*Oliver*	Syd Hoff	89
1.8	*Three by the Sea*	Edward Marshall	137
1.9	*Scruffy*	Peggy Parish	117
1.9	*Stanley*	Syd Hoff	133
2.0	*No Mail for Mitchell*	Catherine Siracusa	81
2.0	*Sammy the Seal*	Syd Hoff	113
2.0	*Smallest Cow in the World*	Katherine Paterson	129
2.1	*The Golly Sisters Go West*	Betsy Byars	45
2.2	*Crocodile and Hen: A Bakongo Folktale*	Joan M. Lexau	33
2.2	*Owl at Home*	Arnold Lobel	97
2.3	*Danny and the Dinosaur*	Syd Hoff	37
2.3	*The Great Snake Escape*	Molly Coxe	49
2.3	*The Horse in Harry's Room*	Syd Hoff	53
2.3	*Little Bear's Visit*	Else Holmelund Minarik	65
2.4	*Aunt Eater Loves a Mystery*	Doug Cushman	5
2.4	*Little Bear*	Else Holmelund Minarik	61
2.4	*Pretty Good Magic*	Cathy East Dubowski and Mark Dubowski	105
2.5	*Mouse Tales*	Arnold Lobel	69
2.5	*Porcupine's Pajama Party*	Terry Webb Harshman	101

2.6	*No Fighting, No Biting*	Else Holmelund Minarik	77
2.6	*Oscar Otter*	Nathaniel Benchley	93
2.6	*R Is for Radish*	Molly Coxe	109
2.7	*Aunt Eater's Mystery Vacation*	Doug Cushman	9
2.7	*The Boston Coffee Party*	Doreen Rappaport	17
2.7	*Buffalo Bill and the Pony Express*	Eleanor Coerr	21
2.8	*Chang's Paper Pony*	Eleanor Coerr	29
2.8	*The Mystery of the Pirate Ghost*	Geoffrey Hayes	73

Index

Items in boldface are books featured in this text.

About the Author

Judy Sauerteig has over thirty years experience teaching in the classroom and working with students in media centers in a variety of environments and capacities. Mrs. Sauerteig has an Elementary Education degree and a Masters in Library Science from the University of Iowa plus numerous hours in related literacy courses. Teaching reading has always been a passion, especially grades one and two. She is the author of *Science to Go: Fact and Fiction Learning Packs*, a book which encourages literacy at home. She lives in Denver, Colorado with her husband and is the Media Coordinator at Cherry Creek Academy Charter School.